COLLATIONS TO NEO-ASSYRIAN LEGAL TEXTS FROM NINEVEH

Simo Parpola
The University of Chicago

Legal texts from the imperial archives of Nineveh are a source of foremost importance not only to the study of the legal practices and economic life of the Neo-Assyrian empire, but above all to the prosopography and chronology of the period. Yet their information potential has never been fully utilized, mainly because the texts can only be consulted through two outdated publications, C.H.W. Johns's *Assyrian Deeds and Documents* and A.Ungnad's and J.Kohler's *Asyrische Rechtsurkunden*. In anticipation of a re-edition of the texts, whose completion still lies years ahead, the present article offers collations to about 300 texts of the corpus providing, besides numerous improvements to the copies of Johns, also a touchstone for earlier collations by Ungnad and others.

As is well known, the excavations of the acropolis of Nineveh produced, among other things, a sizable corpus of Neo-Assyrian legal and administrative documents, most of which were published some 80 years ago by C.H.W. Johns in the first two volumes of his *Assyrian Deeds and Documents* (*ADD*, Cambridge 1898-1901).[1] The legal texts in *ADD* were collated and re-edited in 1913 by Arthur Ungnad in J. Kohler and A. Ungnad, *Assyrische Rechtsurkunden* (*AR*), and in recent times several administrative texts and some legal texts have been re-edited, with collations, by J.N. Postgate, F.M. Fales and others.[2] However, only a few of the texts have been recopied, and consequently the copies of Johns still remain the basic medium

[1] The total number of Neo-Assyrian legal and administrative documents from Nineveh known to the present writer is about 1440, of which some 1135 are included in *ADD* I-II (the round figures are due to the fact that while the texts published in *ADD* are numbered up to 1141, the second volume contains some texts already published in Vol. I as well as fragments that are neither legal nor administrative in character). Later on, 154 more texts were added to the corpus by Johns (23 census lists in Johns, *An Assyrian Doomsday Book* [1901], 130 legal texts in *AJSL* 42 [1926] 170-204 and 228-275, and one temple grant in *AJSL* 44 [1928] 519 ff), and 68 by others (see G. Contenau, *TCL* 9 [1926] 57-66; V. Scheil, *RA* 24 [1927] 111-121; J.N. Postgate, *NARGD* [1969], No. 24; idem, *Iraq* 32 [1970] 129-164 and pls.XVIII-XXXI; idem, *Or* NS 42 [1973] 441-444; F.M. Fales, *CCENA* [1973], No. 23 and fig. 5; idem, *Assur* 1/3 [1974] 5f and 15f; S. Parpola, *ZA* 64 [1974] 96[3]; D. Arnaud, *RA* 69 [1975] 181ff). In addition, there are at least 82 more unpublished fragments of the same type in the Kuyunjik collection of the British Museum, which I hope to find time to publish in the near future.

[2] See Postgate, *NARGD*, *TCAE* (1974) and *FNALD* (1976); Fales, *CCENA* (1973), passim, and *Assur* 1/3 (1974) 6 ff; G. van Driel, *CA* (1969) 206 ff; B. Landsberger, *AfO* Beih.17 (1967) 31f; S. Parpola, *ZA* 65 (1975) 295f; J. V. Kinnier Wilson, *CTN* 1 (1972) 100 ff. Some published collations pertaining only to a single sign of line in *ADD* are omitted here (for these see R. Borger, *HKL* II 118 f), likewise certain unpublished collations by various scholars.

through which these texts have to be utilized in research. In view of the great importance of the texts, this is most unfortunate, for the copies of Johns are not only inaccurate and at times clearly faulty but also, as will be shown in detail below, entirely unreliable.[3] The existence of the collations just mentioned does not significantly improve the situation. Those by Ungnad are only given in transliteration without being explicitly marked as results of collation, so that it is at times impossible to ascertain whether a reading in *AR* deviating from the copy in *ADD* is really based on an inspection of the original or due to some other reason (carelessness, printing error, or the like).[4] Moreover, as indicated by the countless question marks dotting Ungnad's transliterations, inspection of originals often did not lead to definite results, and in not a few cases Ungnad's readings cannot be considered an improvement over Johns'.[5] Many passages in the texts were apparently not collated at all but taken over uncritically from *ADD*,[6] and the transliterations lack the precision which would, in the absence of copies, make it possible for one to form an idea of the lengths of textual breaks, spacing of signs and other similar details bearing on the restoration of broken passages.[7] Such criticism does not apply to the collations by Postgate and Fales, but the texts edited by them are too few to significantly improve the situation.

For these and several other reasons which it is unnecessary to go into here, a comprehensive re-edition of all legal and administrative documents from Nineveh has long been urgently needed. The present article offers itself as a contribution toward this goal, and in the meantime, as an aid to control the copies of Johns and the transliteration of Ungnad. It presents the results of a detailed collation of about 300 *ADD* legal texts during a two-week visit to the British Museum in July/August 1978.[8] The time at my disposal did not suffice for the examination of the whole *ADD* corpus, but there is no question that the remaining texts (particularly the administrative ones) should be subjected to a similar scrutiny. Hopefully this will become possible in the future.

The texts collated were carefully selected to contain the ones presenting the most epigraphic problems among the legal texts. Prior to the collation, a new transliteration of all *ADD* legal texts, based on the copies of Johns checked against the collations of Ungnad and Postgate, was prepared under my direction by Mr. Theodore Kwasman, a student of K. Deller working on a dissertation in the area of Neo-Assyrian legal texts; all unclear or doubtful passages

[3] This rather harsh judgment should not be taken to belittle the value of Johns' work as a whole. At the time of its appearance it marked a giant leap forward and is, despite its shortcomings, in many respects still very useful today.

[4] E.G., in *AR* 466.18, Ungnad reads *be-nu* against *ADD*'s *bé-nu*. Since the former spelling is by far more common in the Neo-Assyrian period, it gives the impression of being the correct one and based on collation. In actual fact, however, the tablet has *bé-nu* as copied by Johns, so Ungnad's reading must be attributed to a printing error or an inaccuracy in the manuscript itself. Similar cases are rather common in *AR* (e.g., *il-ki* often for intended *il-ḳi*).

[5] E.G., in *ADD* 235 r.7, the original does have KUR-*e*, as copied by Johns, not *man.e* (*AR* 231.20 with footnote "Nicht *šad*").

[6] Cf., e.g., *ADD* 328 r.14 = *AR* 357:29, where both Johns and Ungnad read *li-mu* even though the original has a clear *lim-mu*. The former spelling is well attested in MA, but occurs only sporadically in NA texts.

[7] For instance, Ungnad's transliteration does not differentiate between partially preserved signs and signs of uncertain reading, both of which are indicated with a question mark following the sign in question in parentheses. Textual breaks are brushed aside simply as "Lücke" or "grosse Lücke", without any hint as to how many lines or signs are missing; lines are numbered consecutively no matter how many may be missing in the middle of the text; seal impressions, dividing lines, separation marks and the like are consistently left unexpressed, etc.

[8] I wish to thank Dr. E. Sollberger, Keeper and Dr. C.B.F. Walker, Assistant Keeper, for permission to study the tablets, as well as the whole staff of the Department of Western Asiatic Antiquities, especially Mr. K. Upjohn, for the efficient service I enjoyed during my stay. The visit to the Museum was made possible by a travel grant from the research funds of the Oriental Institute, for which I am indebted to the Director of the Institute, Professor J. A. Brinkman.

encountered in the course of this work were noted down, and the relevant texts set aside for collation. Originally, it was my hope that the work with the originals could be limited to the passages thus singled out, but this soon proved to be out of the question. To my surprise, already one of the very first tablets examined by me showed an odd discrepancy between the copy of Johns and the original: the copy twice read LÚ* () where the tablet actually had LÚ (). More similar, even more alarming discrepancies soon emerged, making it necessary to extend the collation to cover every single line in the texts, not just the passages singled out previously. The following selected examples will make the reason behind the discrepancies clear:

TABLET	JOHNS	ATTESTED IN
ad(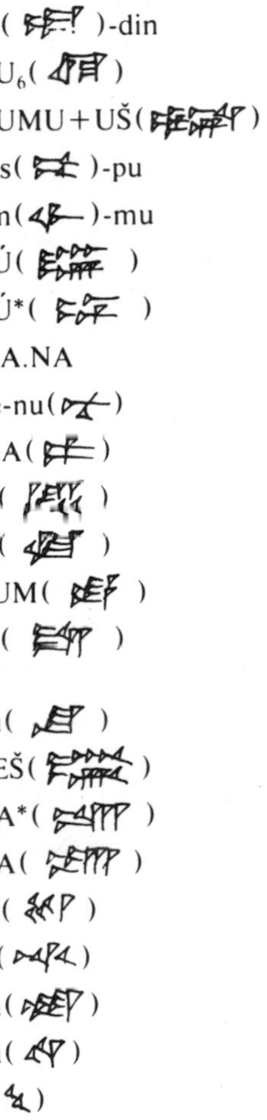)-din	(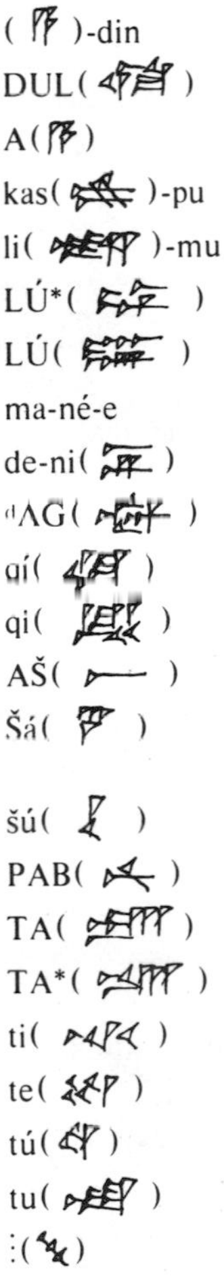)-din	*ADD* 264:4'
DU_6( )	DUL( )	*ADD* 37:4, 75 r.14, 259 r.9, etc.
DUMU+UŠ( )	A( )	*ADD* 208 L.E.1
kás( )-pu	kas( )-pu	*ADD* 384:8,r.6
lim( )-mu	li( )-mu	*ADD* 328 r.14
LÚ( )	LÚ*( )	*ADD* 5 r.4, 420 r.4'
LÚ*( )	LÚ( )	*ADD* 246 r.2 and 8, 279 r.5', etc.
MA.NA	ma-né-e	*ADD* 357:3
de-nu( )	de-ni( )	*ADD* 350:17, 372:2'
ᵈPA( )	ᵈAG( )	*ADD* 242 r.11
qi( )	qí( )	*ADD* 243:11
qí( )	qi( )	*ADD* 351 r.2, 373 r.1 and 3
SUM( )	AŠ( )	*ADD* 420 r.7'
ša( )	šá( )	*ADD* 228 r.1, 255 r.4' -6', *ADD* 258 r.6'
šu( )	šú( )	*ADD* 324 r.7
ŠEŠ( )	PAB( )	*ADD* 350:15
TA*( )	TA( )	*ADD* 179:6, 215:6, and often
TA( )	TA*( )	*ADD* 350:16
te( )	ti( )	*ADD* 257 r.23, 345 r.2'
ti( )	te( )	*ADD* 324 r.8
tu( )	tú( )	*ADD* 265:8'
tú( )	tu( )	*ADD* 86:9'
:( )	:( )	*ADD* 327 r.10 and 11, 352 r.5', etc.

As can be seen, the "copies" of Johns are actually no copies at all but hastily made *transliterations* converted to cuneiform characters without simultaneous consultation of the originals, the occasional omission of diacritic marks resulting in the restitution of a wrong sign in the case of homophonic syllabograms (ša = šá, etc.) or equivalent logograms (ᵈPA = ᵈAG, etc.). While it can be stated that on the whole mistakes of the above kind are relatively rare, the fact nevertheless remains that no single reading in the "copies" (not to speak of the forms of the signs) can be accepted as assured without verification. A scrutiny of the tablets revealed other similar inaccuracies: dividing lines are omitted, or drawn where not actually existent; completely visible signs are omitted; little or no attention is paid to the spacing of signs; textual breaks are misleadingly or incorrectly indicated, mostly by means of square brackets only; seal impressions are not copied and inadequately or totally mistakenly described;[9] "Edge" may occasionally stand for "Left Edge"; fragmentary tablets with lost beginning of the obverse are often not specified as such, etc.

Such inaccuracies may on the whole seem of little significance but taken together they considerably encumber the interpretation of the texts and/or distort the information they offer. More serious is the fact that the "copies" very inaccurately (if at all) reflect the certainty of the readings, so that almost entirely obliterated (and consequently misread) signs not infrequently are presented in the disguise of (almost) prefectly preserved signs, without any indication of doubt whatsoever. Certain misreadings of this type are impossible to detect without consulting the originals—so, for instance, numerous personal names misread by Johns and subsequently entered in standard reference works like K. Tallqvist's *Assyrian Personal Names*; others may strike suspicion, but have nevertheless been quoted in Akkadian grammars and dictionaries as hapax legomena because of their potential correctness.

The list of collations that follows, for practical reason uses *ADD* as a frame of reference, but it also takes a stand on the collations by Ungnad and others, whenever this is necessary. The letter U in parentheses following the collation indicates that the reading of Ungnad has been verified; an asterisked U means that some elements in Ungnad's collation are correct. All square brackets and half-brackets indicate the state of preservation of the tablets at the time of collation. Exclamation marks indicate corrections to the copies of Johns, and generally imply that the reading of the sign in question is certain (though the choice of the syllabic or logographic values may in some cases be open to discussion). Unclear or controversial passages as well as noteworthy sign forms are given in copy. Usually only the portions of text immediately relevant to the collated passage are quoted in transliteration. Comments are kept to a minimum. The system of transliteration in general follows the principles outlined in *AOAT* 5/1 (1970) p. XX, however modified to conform with the system of R. Borger, *Assyrisch-Babylonische Zeichenliste* (1978). Of the special symbols and conventions used, note especially the following:

x	unreadable sign
[.]	break with space for one (or more, indicated by the number of dots) medium-sized sign
O	non-existent sign (where a sign could be expected)
[O]	textual break with space for one sign, probably uninscribed
LÚ*	 (as opposed to LÚ = 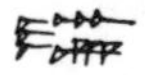)
TA*	 (as opposed to TA = 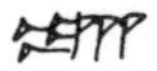)
KAM*	 (as opposed to KÁM  and KAM )
+	ligatured with
: ⁝	ditto marks ( ), occasionally separation mark ()
———	dividing line
[[ ]]	erasure

For the bibliographical abbreviations used see R. Borger *Handbuch der Keilschriftliteratur* II (1975).

[9] For example, *ADD* 433 is sealed with a cylinder seal, not with stamp seals as alleged by Johns; 472 does not have a "space for seals" but is sealed with a cylinder seal; 242, 373, and many others are not sealed at all, contra Johns. While I carefully copied and measured all seal impressions and seal spaces, it would be impractical to publish these data in the present context, and consequently I will here limit myself only to correcting mistakes made by Johns. Hopefully an opportunity will present itself to make the seal drawings and other relevant nontextual data (such as tablet dimensions, script size, line distances, clay color) available in another context.

LIST OF COLLATIONS

ADD 5 (AR 635) Obv 1 ina MA.NA ša! KUR-gar-ga-mis (U*)

2 ša ^{1}za-zi-i [[ina! IGI! $^{1!.d!}$IM!-ba!-]] (erased intentionally)

6 ^{1}ka-ak-ki-ia sic

Edge 8 a-na 3-su-šú sic

9 ^{1}šu- 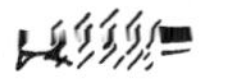 DINGIR

Rev 3 É.GAL SUMUN! (U)

4 LÚ!(not LÚ*)-SIMUG

5 ^{1}ma-an-ki-i LÚ(sic)-: UD.KA.BAR

ADD 7 (AR 284) Obv 2 ša 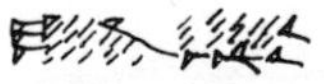

3 ina IGI 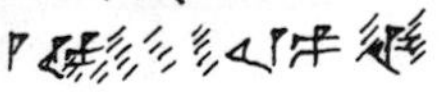

5 [a-n]a [4-t]ú-šú

6 ^{1}U.G[UR]!-DÙ (U)

Rev 2 IGI ^{1}⌜x x x x⌝ (^{1}mil-ki-aš+šur [Johns] excluded)

3 IGI $^{1.d!}$PA-[.]!-GIN

4 name entirely obliterated

5 IT[u-KI]N UD 2⌜2⌝-KAM

ADD 10 (AR 288) Obv 3 ša ^{1}A[Š!

4 ina IGI ^{1}i[m!- (or ^{1}KA[M!-)

Rev 1 lim-mu ^{1} 

2 $^{1.d}$UTU!-⌜da!⌝- 

4 ^{1}a-tan!-[ḫa-DN] (U)

5 $^{1.d}$P[A!-

6 ^{1}BE!-[

ADD 12 (AR 274)	Obv	1	[. . .] KUG.UD ina 1 MA.NA O!
			blank space of 2 lines
		2	[. . . . . L]Ú*-EN.NAM
		4	(end)
	Rev	1	⌜šá⌝ URU-ba!-⌜la!-ṭa!⌝ [. . .]
		4	ina ITU-DU$_6$!(not DUL) i-dan (wr. )
	Edge	7	[IG]I ^{1}EN-ZU O! ^{1}man-nu-ki-NI[NA]
		8	${}^{1.d}$PA-BÀD-EN-⌜iá!⌝
	L.E.	9	[IGI] ^{1}ḫa!-te!-nu!-[.] (U*)
ADD 20 (AR 282)	Obv	1	[NA$_4$-KIŠ]IB! .... 10 GÍN O! KUG.UD SAG.DU
		2	[š]a ^{1}šum-mu!-DINGIR-MEŠ-ni (U)
			————————————————!
			unused space for stamp seal impressions
			————————————————!
		3	^{1}EN-MAŠ!(not SAG.KAL); a-na 4-[t]ú-šú sic
	Rev		Beginning (ca. 8 lines) uninscribed; last line followed by dividing line
ADD 21 (AR 253)	Obv	5	ina! ⌜ITU!-KAN!⌝ [[S]]UM-an
	Rev.	1	ITU-DUL UD-5 sic
		4	^{1}qi-ti-BE sic
ADD 22 (AR 265)	Obv	1	KUG+UD (ligatured)
		2	ša ${}^{1.d!}$A-10-na!-a'-di (U*)
	Edge	8	[^{1}]${}^{.d}$KU-rem-a-ni sic
	Rev	2	^{1}qi!()-ti-DINGIR-MEŠ
		4	^{1}na!()-ni-i
ADD 30 (AR 254)	Obv	5	ITU-DUL sic
	Edge	7	^{1}ḫa-ni-na-ia sic
	Rev	1	^{1}il-lu-uk-nu sic
	Rev	2	^{1}ḫu-ḫa!-na-šu
		4	^{1}am-ma-a sic

ADD 32 (AR 245) Obv 2 LÚ*-GAR!-nu! (U)
6  1 MA.NA
Rev 1 ^{1}E[N-IG]I.LAL-a-ni sic ( ; U: ^{1}[...]-me-a-ni)
2 ^{1}qu[r!-d]i!-URU-KASKAL
3 ^{1}BE!-[.]-PAB!-MEŠ (U*)
4 $^{1.d}$aš+šur!-[a-l]ik!-IGI LÚ*-GAR!-nu! (U*)
5 ^{1}NU[MUN]-u-tú

ADD 36 (AR 242) Obv 1 [NA$_4$-KIŠIB] O! ^{1}ia-a-di-DINGIR
after line 2, dividing line followed by unused seal space

ADD 37 (AR 243) Obv 1 5! MA.NA 6 GÍN LAL (sic) šá gar!-ga!-mis! (U*)
2 ša ^{1}DÙG!-É-15
4 ITU-DU$_6$! (not DUL)
Rev 2 ^{1}qí-bit-DINGIR! (U)
3 ^{1}U+G[UR]-I sic ()

ADD 44 (AR 295) Obv 3 NINDA-MEŠ sic
Rev 1 ^{1}si-lim-⌜aš+šur⌝ possible
2 $^{1.d}$[.]-šal!-lim!
3 ^{1}⌜x x⌝-ba!-
4 ^{1}ú-bu-⌜qu⌝ sic ()
Edge 6 ^{1}ḫa!-nu-nu! (U)
7 IGI! $^{1!}$[. . .]
L.E. 8 ITU-D[UL . . .]
9 lim-mu ^{1}DI-mu-EN-Ḫ[AL]

ADD 45 (AR 272) Rev 4 IGI ^{1}EN-MAN-DÙ IGI ^{1} 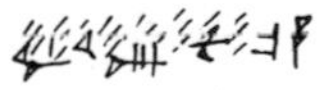
5 IGI ^{1}⌜x x⌝ (unreadable; Marduk-ibni excluded)
6 name unreadable
Edge 7 $^{1.d}$IM-A-⌜x x⌝ (Johns' "SUM-ni" excluded)

ADD 47 (AR 251) Obv 5 [G]AL!-⌜É!⌝ ša SUKKAL-MEŠ
6 [. . .] MA.NA ⌜x x x⌝ (not i-rab-bi)
Rev 1! [. . . . -K]AM!
2! O! lim-mu ^{1}man-nu-ki-10 (U)
Rev 3' IGI! $^{1!}$MAN LÚ*-NAR (U; sic)

ADD 51 (AR 252)	Obv 1	[N]A$_4$-KIŠIB
	2	ina 1 MA.NA-e! šá! [.] (U)
		unused space for stamp seals
	Rev 3	(end) IGI ^{1}URU!-zab!-
ADD 52 (AR 276)	Obv 1	ki-[ṣir]-⸢te⸣
	2	[ina 1 MA.NA-e] ⸢šá⸣ U[RU-g]ar-ga-mis
	10	ITU-AB UD-10!-KAM* lim-mu [. . . .] (U)
	Rev 1	IGI $^{1.d}$UTU- A[Š]
		unused space for stamp seals
ADD 53 (AR 258)	Obv 1'	ù du
	3'	ina SAG.DU DINGIR GIBIL! ⸢šá⸣ IT[U!
	7'	^{1}PAB-DU-ka sic
ADD 54 (AR 244)	Obv 1'	now entirely lost
	2'	^{1}BÀD-PAB!-M[EŠ!-š]ú!
	Rev 5	[. . .] -i ṣa-bit e!-gí[r!-te]
	6	[ITU-MN UD-] -KÁM*! (not -KAM)
	7!	[. . . . .]!
ADD 55 (AR 247)	Obv 1!	vitrified and illegible
	2!	[ina 1 MA.NA-e]! ⸢šá!⸣ URU-gar-ga-mis
	3!	[ša] ^{1}A-[ia] ina IGI O! (U)
	4!	[^{1}]EN-A- [. .]
	6!	2 [GÍN]-MEŠ ina [MA].NA š[a IT]U-šú
	Edge 7!	i-⸢ra⸣-[ab]-bi
	8!	ITU-DUL(sic) UD-[.]-KAM
	Rev 1	l[im-mu ^{1}]$^{.d}$PA-GIN-PAB
	2	IGI [^{1}D]INGIR!-ḫa!-na!-ni (U*)
	5	[IGI ^{1}] -⸢sa⸣-gab (1 sign only between 1 and sa)
ADD 56 (AR 639)	Obv 1'	[. . . .] [ ]
	2'	[. . . .] šum-ma la ⸢i⸣-[din]
		cylinder seal impression (not followed by ruling)
	5'	[^{1}. . .]-15! TA* (U)

ADD 56 (AR 639) Rev 7 [. . . . . .] IGI $^{1.d}$PA- 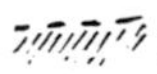 LÚ*- 
traces of two more broken lines

ADD 57 (AR 263) Obv 1 [.] ⌜x x⌝ KUG.UD (x x hardly = GÍN-MEŠ)
2 [. . .] 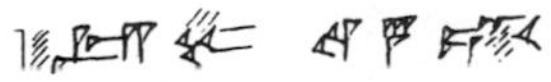
4 [ina IGI ^{1}]GÌR+2!-15
5 [ina SA]G.DU (U)
6 [ša] ITU-DUL sic
Edge 7 [šum-m]a
8 [a-na] 3-si-šú
Rev 2 [lim-mu]!
3 [IGI ^{1}]ÚR!-15 (U*)
7 [IGI ^{1}.]-nu-ni-ia sic

ADD 59 (AR 123) Obv 3 followed by dividing line, unused space for stamp seal impressions, and another dividing line
6 ^{1}dul!-la-a-a-qa-nun (U)
10 URU-da!-di-ú-al-la
11 ina EN.NAM URU-ri-mu-si sic
13 šá [ur-k]iš u! ma-te-ma (U*)
16 [lu-u D]UMU-šú (U)
17 [GIL-u-ni . MA.N]A KUG.UD ina ⌜bur-ki⌝ [. . . . . .] (U)
about 5 lines lost at end of Obverse
about 10 lines lost at beginning of Reverse
Rev 1' IGI ^{1}⌜ú!⌝-  . . . .]

ADD 60 (AR 153) Obv 2 [NA_4-KIŠIB ^{1}]⌜I!⌝-^{d}MAŠ LÚ-da-gil-a![(U)
4 at end space for šá-pa[r-ti ina IGI ^{1}rém-a-ni-^{d}IM] (U)
————————————————————————!
unused space for stamp seal impressions
————————————————————————!
5 LÚ-DIB-KUŠ-PA-MEŠ dan-nu šá LUGA[L! šá-kín]
Edge 12 $^{1.d}$PA-NUMUN!-AŠ (U)
Rev 3 followed by dividing line, unused space for stamp seal impressions, and another dividing line
6 [IGI ^{1}. .]-AŠ! LU-⌜:!⌝
8 [ITU-MN UD-  -KÁM lim-me ^{1}ITU-AB-a-[a]
9 (end) LÚ-A.BA šá 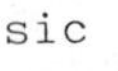

ADD 62 (AR 131) Obv 2 ^{1}i-ni-bi-aš+šur sic (Postgate TCAE p.303: ^{1}in-bi-)
5 še-e[b]-šu ŠE-nu-sa-ḫi
6 ú-sa-ni-lum sic (thus also Rev.2)

ADD 62 (AR 131)	Obv	8	[. . . . .]-ḫi ur!-ta-me! (Postgate)
		9	[. . . . .] $^{1!}$PAB-SU
	Rev	1	[. . . . .] ku!-um! ŠE-nu-sa-ḫi (Postgate)
		2	šá ú-sa-ni-lum
		5	a-de-e ša ŠU+2-šú sic
		6	IGI ^{1}kab!-lu!-15 ( ); last name illegible
ADD 63 (AR 126)	Obv	3	[ina] IGI ^{1}[man-nu]-ki!-LÚ-ERIM (U)
			very faint impression of stamp(?) seal, no rulings
		4	[ina]! ku-um
		5	[ina]! ⌜šá⌝-bar-ti
		6	[ina] UD-me
	Rev	1	[Ú]Š ḫal-qa sic
		6	IGI ^{1}
		7	IGI ^{1} -e
		8	[IGI ^{1}] -ti-e
ADD 64 (AR 152)	Obv	1	[NA$_{4}$-KIŠIB ^{1}.]-DÙG+GA! LÚ*-2- ⌜i?⌝ (U)
			3 impressions of stamp seal, no rulings
		3	ta-da-an sic
		4	⌜É!⌝ 2 me
		13	a-ar-šú sic
	Edge	14	ina! ku-⌜mu⌝ 15 MA.NA ⌜KUG.UD⌝ (U)
		15	ina 1 MA.[NA š]a
	Rev	1	ina IGI ^{1}KALAG!-an-na!-a-a! ( )
		2	ši-par!-ti
		3	šá-ki!-an! man-nu!
		4	š[a! . . .] ú-še-ra-ba-an-ni
		8	^{1}da-ru-ra-a sic
		9	^{1}ḫa-ra- MAN sic (not -U.U; but cf. below, ADD 387 r4')
		11	^{1}ḫa-ba-a-si-te-ma!
		12	^{1}za-ib-da-a-ni sic (cf. r3)
		14	lim O! $^{1.d}$PA-U-PAB
		15!	ki-ṣir $^{1.d}$aš+šur!( )-PAB-AŠ (U*; whole line omitted in ADD)
		16!	[MAN] KUR-aš+šur (U)
ADD 67 (AR 125)	Obv	1	ma-né-e URU!-gar!-gar!-mis! ( )
		2	[ša MÍ-š]á!-ki-in-ti (U)
		3	⌜ina! x⌝ URUDU! ( )

ADD 67 (AR 125) Obv 8 šá MURUB$_{4}$-URU kam!-mu!-⸢su!⸣
9 ina A!-MEŠ! ina! Ì!-MEŠ! ina! ZÁḪ ina ÚŠ!
10 ina MUŠ! ina! GÍR! ina UGU ^{1} 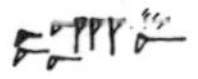
Rev 1 MÍ-šá-ki-in-tú KUG.UD-šá 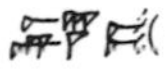(for expected tadaggal)
2 [UD]-mu ša KUG.UD ⸢SUM-ni⸣ LÚ* ú-š[e]-ṣ[a]
3 ⸢šúm⸣-mu  la 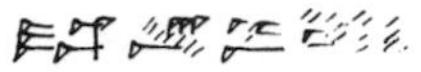
4 ⸢MÍ⸣-šá-[ki]-in-tú KUG.UD-⸢šá!⸣
6 IGI ^{1}BE!()-a
Edge 9 [IGI ^{1}] su-ma!-a-a A!.[BA]
10 [IT]U-KAN! UD-26-KAM*!(not KÁM)
L.E. 11 lim-mu 1-$^{d!}$30-MU!-DÙ? ()

ADD 68 (AR 112) Obv 3 ^{1}muš-ke-nu-la!-ŠEŠ
4 ^{1}LAL-KAL!-15 (U) sic
5  (for LÚ-Ì.ŠUR ?)
Edge 8 ṭup-⸢pu!⸣-šú
9 ki-ma-a (sic) ṭup-pi-šú 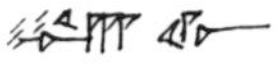
Rev 4 ina muḫ-ḫi! EN-šú (U)
5 UD-13! (U)
Edge 7 ^{1}ur-ri-ḫa sic
9 IGI ^{1}da!-ia-[.]!
L.E.10 ^{1}qi-te-NU sic
11 ^{1}SUḪUŠ()-DI.KUD!
12 ^{1}ra-man-ra-[me]!

ADD 69 (AR 134) Obv 1 followed by dividing line, impression of stamp seal, and another dividing line
2 [. . KUG.UD š]a
4 URU-šú(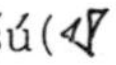)-ra sic
6 [IGI ^{1}].$^{d!}$30-MAN-PAB
7 [IGI ^{1}].⸢^{d}⸣UTU-ú-pa-ḫír
blank space of two lines
9 [ ]!-a

ADD 70 (AR 115) Obv 1! [NA$_{4}$-KIŠIB . .] ina! KUR-ḫa-zi!-te
2! [DUMU ^{1}.(.)-m]ur!-DINGIR (U*)
3! [E]N A.ŠÀ SUM-ni
――――――――――――――――!
stamp seal impressions
――――――――――――――――!
4! É 3! ANŠE! (with overwritten 4BÁN) A.Š[À ()
7! [SUḪUR ^{1}DING]IR!-⸢a!⸣-[a-. . .]

ADD 70 (AR 115) Rev 1 [U]RU!-ši-[.] [. .]
2 ina mu!-le!-e! [Ọ]
4 ŠE-ši-ib-še l[a! . . .]
5 URU-bar-ú-ri! ( )
8 šá-par!-[ti (U*)
Edge 11 followed by dividing line
12! IGI ^{1}si-lim-aš+šur! IGI! ^{1}di!-di!-a! (U*; = Johns' "Obv.1")
13! [IGI ^{1}pal-ḫ]u!-ú!-še-zib! (U*)
L.E. 15 URU-bar-ú-ri! ( )
16 [IGI ^{1}. .]-AŠ! A.BA! ITU-SIG$_4$ (U*)
17 KUR-bar-ḫal-⸢zi!⸣ (U*)

ADD 72 (AR 129) Obv 1 followed by dividing line, (unused?) space for stamp seal impressions, and another dividing line
4 [. . . . . .]⸢r⸣ig! ( )
5 šap-ri sic
6 [kam-m]u-sat (U*)
7 0! [S]UM-an (contra U, no space for KUG.UD)
12 [LÚ*]!-SUKKAL [GAL]-ú!
Rev 8 followed by double ruling

ADD 73 (AR 137) Rev 6 IGI ^{1}lu-u-ba-laṭ IGI ^{1}⸢la!⸣-tú!-ba!-0
L.E.10 ⸢ŠU!⸣ UD!-6!-KAM! (U*)

ADD 74 (AR 138) Obv 3 followed by cylinder seal impression
5 kal-e sic
Rev 2 $^{1.d}$PA-SIG!-DINGIR-MEŠ (U)
3 ^{1}a-bi-da-nu (no -a- after da-)
L.E.10 EGIR da!-⸢ra!-ri!⸣ (cf. ADD 310:11; Postgate FNALD p.24 reads da-aḫ-ri)
11 U[D!-. .]
12 [. .]

ADD 75 (AR 652) Obv 2 [ṣu-pur ^{1}. .]-i [. . .]!
- - - - - - ——— - - -!
fingernail impression
- - - - - - ——— - - -!
3 [. . . . . . .] r[a! . . .]
4 [. . . . .] a a [. .]!
10 [. . . . .] SAG! (U)
Rev 7 ^{1}mu-šal-lim-^{d}+INNIN! (U)

ADD 75 (AR 652) Rev 11 $^{1.d}$30-AŠ LÚ-3!.U$_5$! (U)
13 [^{1}i]m-ma-ni-aš+šur sic
14 URU-DU$_6$!(not DUL)-^{d}MAŠ-a-a
16 LÚ-ÌR-MEŠ ša LÚ-[GAL]-SA[G]!
18 [ITU-Z]ÍZ UD-26-KAM (U)
19 [$^{1.d}$P]A!-⸢KALAG⸣-in-an-ni

ADD 77 (AR 133) Obv 1 [. . . . . .] URU!-kal!-ḫi! PAB! 2!
6 [ša ^{1}lu-š]á-kin
7 [lu-u LÚ*-E]N!.NAM-su
Rev 2' [IGI ^{1}. . .]-ir! DUMU ^{1}lu-DI-me

ADD 79 (AR 130) Obv 1 [. . .]⸢x x⸣ÌR ⸢šá⸣ ^{1}tar-ḫu- [. . .]
2 PAB 4 LÚ-ZI-M[EŠ]!
3 [a-na šá-par-ti GA]R!-nu
7 [id-dan šum-m]a! ... ^{1}ti-U[R!-a-me]
8 laq-qi-ú . .]
!
9 [. . . . . . .] $^{1.d}$PA-MU-PAB [. . .]!

ADD 80 (AR 640) Obv 3 DUMU ^{1}15-⸢I!⸣
4 A ^{1}lu-GAR O!
5 KUŠ-maš-kur$_4$ ša 16! GÍD.DA
6 ku-me ina! ITU-GUD O!
no dividing line after Obv 7
Rev 1 EN-ŠU+2-[MEŠ]! O!
3 LÚ*-[. .]
Edge 6 $^{1.d}$PA-⸢u+a⸣ (ligatured)

ADD 81 (AR 117) Obv 1 ^{d}15 ⸢arba+ìl⸣-KI! or ^{d}15 šá! ⸢NINA!⸣-KI! ( )
6 inserted between lines in smaller script
7 ḫar-pu-tú!
8 za-ku-tú! ⸢šú⸣-nu (small script)
9 ^{1}kaš-šu-[d]u!
Edge 10 ^{1}kaš-šu-d[i]!
11 SUḪUR KASKAL! 3! MU!.AN!-⸢MEŠ⸣ (sic; cf. r1)

ADD 82 (AR 117a) Obv 4 [(.). . 11] GÍN-MEŠ
5! [ina IGI] ⸢^{1}GÌR!-15!⸣ [. . .]
Rev! 1' [IGI ^{1}. .] ⸢IGI! $^{1!}$GÌR!-15! IGI! $^{1!}$⸣]
2' [IGI ^{1}O!]15-ÚŠ-tú-bal-liṭ

ADD 85 (AR 656) Obv 1 [. . .] ^{1}man-nu-ki-i!-^{d}MA[Š]! (U om. -i-)

2 [. . . KUG].UD ḫa!-bu-li-š[u] sic (U: ḫu-)

3 [$^{1.d}$NU-M]AN!-iq-bi

4 i[d!-di]n! (U; no space for i[t-ti-di]n)

5 followed by dividing line, unused space for stamp seal impressions, and another dividing line

6 TA*!(not TA) IGI

Edge 9 [lu-u . . . .] -šu

Rev 1 $^{1.d}$NU-MAN-DUG$_4$.GA!

2 UD-16!-KAM*

5 [. . . . . . .] . . .]

7 [0! IGI ^{1}i]m-ma-ni-[DINGIR . . .]!

ADD 86 (AR 43) Obv Beginning destroyed, then seal space with stamp seal impression

——————————————!

1' ⌜^{MÍ}NIN⌝-AD-šá DUMU.MÍ-s[u]

2' SUḪUŠ wr.

5' ku!-um! 30 GÍN-MEŠ KUG.UD ⌜il!⌝-q[í]!

6' ⌜šá!⌝ ^{1}za-ab-di-i šá (obliterated, over edge)

8' ^{1}zab-di-⌜i!⌝ (U)

9' šu-a-tú! (not -tu)

10' [la]q!-qi-at (U)

11' [tu]-⌜a!-ru!⌝ [d]e-⌜e!⌝-nu

12' u]r!-kiš

Rev 1'! [.] x [.]x ⌜de!⌝-e!-nu! ⌜DUG$_4$⌝!.D[UG$_4$]!

6'! 10-MEŠ-[te]!

10'! ^{1}aš+šur-MU-LAL-[.]!

11'! [IGI] ^{1}mu!-qu-[.]

13'! [IGI ^{1}]10-mil-ki-[. . .]! ( )

L.E.1-2 virtually illegible; witnesses

3 ITU-ŠU UD-⌜x-KAM⌝ [lim-me] ^{1}⌜aš+šur⌝-BÀD-PAB

ADD 90 (AR 128) Collated by Postgate, FNALD no.39; my readings agree with his, except for the following:

Rev 10 [IGI] $^{1.d!}$PA!-[. . .]

In Rev.3, the tablet appears to read LÚ*-ERIM ITU, probably a mistake for EGIR ITU (thus U & Postgate)

ADD 91 (AR 156) Obv 2' [. . . .]⌜x⌝[L]Ú-ZI-MEŠ [. .]!

Edge 5' [. . . . .] ina qa-ni a!-[. . .]

ADD 92 (AR 239) Obv 3 ^{MÍ}DI!-mu-i-tú (U)

5 URU-⌜ni!⌝-[. . .]

stamp seal impression (without a dividing line preceding)

Rev 6' ^{1}ku-lu-ka-a[n!-. .]

ADD 94 (AR 230) Obv 1! [. . . . .] [. . . .]

2! [. . . . .] [. . . .]

3! [. . . . .]

(unused?) seal space

———————————————!

4! [. . . . $^{1.d}$P]A!-u-a

5! [SUM]!-⌜an! BE⌝-ma la kit-tú (sic) la SUM-ni

8! šá LU!

Rev 2 [IGI ^{1}]gu-gu-⌜ú!⌝ [. . .-a]-a

3 [IGI] ^{1}AD- (blank) [. .]

5 lim-m[u . . .]!

6 [0]! (blank) LÚ-[. . .]

ADD 95 (AR 661) Obv 2 [. . . . .] -ti!

3 [. . . . . .]-'bi' ina! qa!(sic) URUDU-MEŠ

——————————————————————!

unused space for finger-nail impressions

——————————————————————!

4 [. . . . .] ⌜ú!⌝-pe-e

6 [. . . . . . .]

Rev 1 [. . . . . . .]-⌜i!⌝

2 [. . . . . .-M]EŠ!-ni

3 [IGI ^{1} . .]-⌜a!⌝-a

4 [IGI ^{1} . .]-⌜a!⌝-nu

5 [ITU-. UD-.-KAM lim]-mu (room enough for month & day!)

ADD 96 + ADD 170 (AR 662 + AR 647)

Obv 1 de-nu ša ^{d}I[M!. .]

2 ša URU- [. .(.)]

3 e-me-du-u-n[i . .(.)]

4 4 GÍN-MEŠ [KUG.UD]

5 ša ^{1}NUMUN!-[. . .]

Edge 6 ina IGI $^{1.d}$UT[U!-. .]

7 ina UD-5!-KAM* [ša ITU-.)

8 KUG.UD ú-š[al!-lam]

Rev 1 i-dan šúm-m[a la i-din]

ADD 96 + ADD 170 (AR 662 + AR 647)			
	Rev	2	a-na ½ GÍ[N-šú GAL-bi]
			space with stamp seal impression
	Edge	3	ITU-GUD UD-20-KA[M*]
		4	lim-mu ^{1}aš+šur-DINGIR-a-⸢a⸣
		5	IGI ^{1}A+10!-BE-PAB-MEŠ (U)
		6	IGI $^{1.d}$ŠÚ-MAN!-PAB (U)
	L.E.	7	IGI $^{1.d}$PA-NUMUN-AŠ
		8	IGI ^{1}rém-a-ni-15! (U)
		9	IGI ^{1}A+10-id-ri
ADD 97 (AR 663)	Obv		illegible
	Edge	1'	[ITU-GU]D UD-16-[KAM . . . .]!
	Rev	2	^{1}ú-a- [. . .]
		3	this line does not exist
		4	$^{1.d}$PA-ka-ṣ[ir . .]!
		5	^{1}ur-ki-me-⸢e⸣[. . .]!
		6	^{1} -na-a-[a . . .]!
	Edge	7	^{1}ba!-⸢x⸣[. .]
ADD 98 (AR 229)	Obv	1	[. . . .] šá! ITU-SIG$_{4}$
		2	[. . .]! šá ^{1}ú-qu-pu (U)
		3	[ina ŠU]+2 ^{1}me-na-ḫi-me
		4	la ú-sa-ḫir! ( )
	Rev	6	[lim-mu] ^{1}aš+šur-gar-ru-u!+a-ni-ri
	Edge	7	[IGI $^{1.d}$+A]G!-MAN-PAB-MEŠ-šú
		8	[. .(.)] -at
ADD 100 (AR 636)	Obv	3	^{1}ÌR-ia-ar-da!-a (U*)
		4	$^{1!}$mu!-na!-bi-du (U)
		7	^{1}ÌR-ia-ar-da!-a (U*)
	Rev	5	ITU-DUL(sic) UD- -KAM
ADD 101 (AR 642)	Case	1	[ ] ITU-S[IG$_{4}$! (U*)
		2	[^{1}pu-ḫ]ur!-GIŠ ^{1}EN-GIN-[(U*)
		3	[IGI-MEŠ-šú] ú!-ba-la
	Obv	1	[. . . .] ITU-S[IG$_{4}$! . . . .]
		3	^{1}[. . .] ^{1}pu!-ḫur-[GIŠ . .]
		5	ú-ka-nu ki-i 37! [. . .] (U)
		6	a-na ^{1}m[u!-tak-kil-aš+šur]

ADD 101 (AR 642) Obv 7 i-din-u-ni  . . . .]
Rev 1 šu-u $^{1.d}$MAŠ-PAB-PAB [. .]! (U*)
2 šum-ma IGI-MEŠ i-⌜tu!⌝-[bi-la] sic (U: i-bil-[..])
3 KUG.UD a-di ru-bé-šú $^{1.⌜d!⌝}$[MAŠ-PAB-PAB]

ADD 102 Obv 2 A ^{1}IGI!-^{d}PA-ṭè-mì (Postgate, FNALD p.160)
4 ina [qa]b-si ⌜ni⌝-nu-u-a a!-na! (Postgate,ibid.)
impression of a circular stamp seal (over ll. 5-7)
9 ša GÉME! ⌜ša!⌝ iq!-b[u]!-⌜u!⌝-ni
Edge 10 ma-a LÚ*!(not LÚ)-ur-ki-i i-ba!-áš-ši
Rev 1 ú-bal-la la 
4 la ú-ma-ṭí ur-ta-me!-šu! O!
5 a-ki-ma i-ṣa-du-šú !
L.E. 10 IGI ^{1}pa!-šá-nu (Postgate. l.c.)

ADD 103 (AR 241) Obv 4 URU-[s]u-pu-ri-e-di-te sic
5 [^{M}]^{I}NIN!-[s]u!-nu MÍ-[TUR]-su
Edge 6 ina ITU-SIG$_4$ [ina KUG.UD] i-dan
7 [šú]m!-mu! MÍ!-T[U]R!-su! (U*)
Rev 4 [šú]m-mu i-ti-din
5 [KUG.UD] ⌜gab⌝-bu-ma  (= ta-din ?)

ADD 109 (AR 275) Obv 1 [. .] KUG.UD
2 [. . . ^{1}]$^{.d}$AMAR.UTU-ŠEŠ A! [. . .]
3 [. . . .] UD-15-KAM*
4 [. ma-n]é!-e
———————————!
Rev 1' [. . .] KUR-NIM.MA [. . . .]
remainder uninscribed(!)

ADD 110 (AR 278) Obv 2 [.(.) G]IŠ!-APIN sic
3 [. . . .] ša ^{1}si-niq-15
4 [. . . .] ⌜it!⌝-tu-ra
Rev 1' [. . . .] ḫi-bi-⌜la!⌝-[te]
2' [. .(.)] ŠU+2! ^{1}si-niq-15
3' [. .-b]i!-⌜lu!⌝-u-ni

ADD 111 (AR 277) Obv! 1 [. . . MA].NA KUG.UD
2 [sa ^{1}.]-lu-KI/DI ()
3 [ina IGI ^{1}]dan!-ni-i (U)

ADD 111 (AR 277)	Obv!	4	[a-na 4]-⸢tú!⸣ GAL
		5	[ITU-.] UD-4 [0]!
	Edge	6	[lim-mu ^{1}]EN-[.]
	Rev!	1	[IGI $^{1.d}$A]G!-
		3	[IGI ^{1}qu]r!-di-10
		4	[IGI ^{1}š]um!-ma-ia-u!
ADD 112 (AR 235)	Obv	1	[. . .]-MEŠ 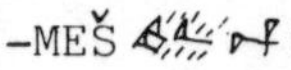 UGU É
		2	^{1}šúm-ma-DINGIR-MEŠ :  qa-bu!-u!-⸢ni⸣
		4	TA*(not TA) IGI LÚ*!(not LÚ)-NAR-MEŠ
		6	šal!-lu-mu SUM-ni
	Rev	2	0! LÚ*-šá-UGU-qa!-a!-te
		4	IGI ^{1}se-e'!-lu! 0!
		5	[IGI$^{1.d}$]šá!-maš!-ÁG-ZI
		6	[IGI ^{1}. .]-SU LÚ*-mu-ḪAL!(not -tar) ANŠE! (
		7	[IGI ^{1}a-n]a!-aš+šur-tak-lak
ADD 113 (AR 637)	Obv	5	⸢a!⸣-na! ITU-KIN
		7	[KUG.UD! ina] ⸢½⸣
	Rev	1	[IGI]$^{⸢1!.d!⸣}$PA-la-tú-šar-a-ni
		4	^{1}sa-la-ma-me sic
		6	ITU-SIG_4 [0]!
ADD 118 (AR 315)	Obv	1	^{1}ia-ḫu-ṭi sic
		3	followed by blank space of about 3 lines
		6	^{1}DINGIR-DU-[. . . . . (.)]
	Rev	1	^{1}ba-ṭu-ṭa-[nu] LÚ-0!-A.[BA]!
		4	followed by blank space of about 3 lines
ADD 119 (AR 221)	Obv	1	ša ^{1}si!-lim!-⸢aš+šur!⸣
		2	 (sic!)
		4	followed by blank space of 1 line
	Edge	7	[a-na mi]t-ḫar 
	Rev	1	[^{1}]⸢EN⸣-APIN
		4	^{1}bi-⸢li!⸣-i
	L.E.	2	this line does not exist
ADD 121 (AR 226)	Rev	1	[. . .]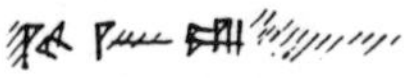
		2	[. . a-na] mit-ḫar ⸢x⸣[. . .]
		3	ITU-B[ARAG U]D-1 li-mu (sic)

ADD 126 (AR 638) Obv 1 NA$_{4}$-KI[ŠIB ^{1}s]i!-me!-[s]i!-me (U*)
2 LÚ-GAL-URU-MEŠ šá 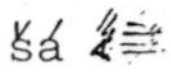 -⌜a⌝-ḫu-si-te (sic)
3 5 ANŠE 2BÁN! GEŠTIN-[0]-MEŠ
4 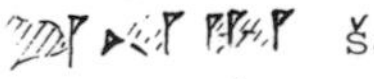 šá ^{1}⌜si⌝-lim-aš+šur
5 ina IGI ^{1}si-⌜me!-si!⌝-⌞i⌟-me
7 ^{1}me-eḫ-sa-a (sic) ⌜EN!⌝-Š[U+2]-MEŠ! (U)
Rev 1 ^{1}PAB-BÀD! (U)

ADD 130 (AR 327) Upper edge: impression of square stamp seal

ADD 133 (AR 307) Obv 3 followed by impression of cylinder seal; no rulings
Rev 1 ITU-ŠU 23! (U)

ADD 135 (AR 236) Rev 3 ITU-DU$_{6}$! 0!

ADD 137 (AR 318) Obv 3 LÚ*-GA[L-kar-ma-ni]
5 followed by two stamp seal impressions
6 [.]  SUM-an
break
Rev two stamp seal impressions
1' [[IGI]]! (blank)
2' IGI ^{1}te-RIG!()-[. .]
3' IGI ^{1}LUGAL-⌜DINGIR!-a!⌝-[a . .]
4' IGI ^{1}qur!-[di-. .]
one line blank
6' IGI $^{1.d}$PA-šá!-ri[d! . . .]

ADD 138 (AR 328) Obv 3 ^{1}še!-x[. . .] ()
4 ^{1}ÌR!-1[5!. .]
8 ^{1}SU!-DINGIR-MEŠ-ni (U)
stamp seal impression (on top of Rev.!)

ADD 146 (AR 290) Obv 2' ina IGI $^{1.d}$[. .]-⌜a!⌝ 0!
4' ša URU-d[u]!-⌜ú!⌝-'a
Rev 1 ITU-BARAG UD-26!
remainder destroyed

ADD 147 (AR 324) Obv 1 ŠE!-šu-'i
3 ina IGI ^{1}EN-ku!-u (U)
4 URU-ar-ga-su!
Edge 9 ^{1}EN-KUR-(space)u+a! (cf r5)

ADD 147 (AR 324)	Rev 3	ŠE!-šu-'i
	5	IGI ^{1}ri-mu-(space)-u+a!
	Edge 7	IGI ^{1}⌜ba!-si!-⌝i!
	8	IGI ^{1}⌜šá!⌝-kil!-ia
ADD 148 (AR 325)	Obv 1	3 ANŠE ŠE-GIG O! (no MEŠ!)
	2	ina GIŠ-BÁN ša!(not šá)
	3	^{1}a-du-ni-iḫ-a sic
	Rev 3	a-na 1! ANŠE 5BÁN GAL-a! (U; written 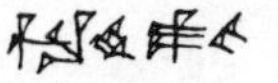)
	L.E.!	= Johns' "Edge"
ADD 152 (AR 653)	Obv 5	ša URU-ba!-la!-MEŠ
	8	ša MAN ša sic
	Rev 1	LÚ*-ša!-ZAG (U; sic)
	6	URU-na-ṣa-pi-na-a-a sic
ADD 153 (AR 228)	Obv 1	UD-22!-KAM (U)
	Rev 2	^{1}bu-si-DINGIR-M[E]Š!
	3	ša!-IGI-de-na-ni (U)
	4	[^{1}]-⌜ú⌝-bu-ra-⌜ki⌝ sic
	5	^{1}[mu]-ni-e-pu-uš-DINGIR
	6	$^{1.d}$PA-BÀD-EN sic
	7	$^{1.d}$PA-(space)u+a!
ADD 154 (AR 227)	Obv 1	NA$_4$-KIŠIB ^{1}DIL-šal-lim [. . .]-A-PAB sic (U wrongly)
	2	UD-32!-KAM (sic!)
	5	^{1}gab!-[b]u!-ŠU+2-DINGIR (U*)
	6	la na-ṣa la! SUM-ni (U)
	7	[ÌR] ša a-ki Ì[R]-⌜i⌝-šú (U wrongly a-ki-i)
	8	[SUM]-an! ITU-GUD UD-⌜26!⌝ O (no KAM!)
	12	sic
	13	[I]GI $^{1.}$⌜$^{d!}$NIN!.URTA!-KAR!-a!-⌝ni!
	14	sic
	15	[IIGI] $^{1.d}$PA-u+a!
ADD 159 (AR 665)	Rev! 1'	[IGI] $^{1!}$pi!-pi-ia [...]
	2'	[IGI] $^{1!}$bar-na!-pi-i [. .] (U)
	3'	[IGI ^{1}]áš-ta-ma-áš-ti [. . .] sic
	5'	IG[I ^{1}g]ab-bu-DINGIR-MEŠ-KAM!-[eš] (preceded by a blank line)

Text	Line	Reading
ADD 161 (AR 51)		Collated by Postgate, FNALD p.162 f. My readings agree with his, except for
	Obv 6	URUDU-MEŠ TA*!(issi)-si (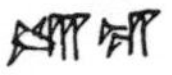), for issisi (sasû Pf.)
ADD 163 (AR 182)	Obv 2	TA*! ^{1}ṣal-mu-PAB-MEŠ
	4	followed by two stamp seal impressions, no rulings
	Edge 6	LÚ-TIN sic (thus also in 1.8)
	Rev 3	⌜DI!-mu!⌝ ina ⌜bir!⌝-tú!-šú!-nu! <ša> GIL-u-ni
	4	aš+šur ^{d}⌜UTU!⌝ EN de-ni-šú
	5	$^{d!}$aš+šur! [x] EN ()
	7	^{1}li-pu-su sic
	9	^{1}SUḪUŠ-^{d}PA O! ^{1}la-qe-pu
	10	^{1}il-qi-su sic
ADD 165 (AR 645)	Obv 2	^{1}mal-ga-d[i! . . .] (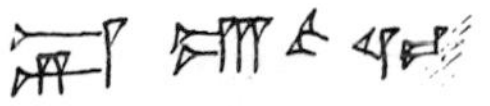)
	3	^{1}pa-ši-i di-[. . .]
		two circular stamp seal impressions, no rulings
	7	[. . . . .] ⌜ti!⌝ [. . . .]
	Rev 12	^{1}du-nu-
	L.E. 5	IGI! $^{1!}$ḫu!-zi-ru!
ADD 166 (AR 644)	Obv 1	$^{1.d}$PA-PAB-MEŠ-S[UM!-na]
	3	followed by two stamp seal impressions, no rulings
	Edge 7	-um written DUB (thus also in Rev.4)
	Rev 3	a-di ŠÀ! ITU-AB
	5	a-na 1 ka-nu-ni sic
	Edge 8	(end) ^{1}ÌR!-DÙ!-tú
	L.E. 1	ITU-[.] UD-19! ⌜šá!⌝
	2	lim-mu ^{1} 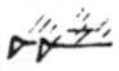 -MAN- 
ADD 167 (AR 223)	Edge	possibly obliterated but looks like blank
	Obv 1!=	Johns' Obv."2"
	5!	ša! É!-šú
	Rev 3	^{1}mu-sa-la-me! (U) sic
	4	^{1}na!-mu-u (U) sic
ADD 168 (AR 651)	Obv 1	[de-e-nu ša] SUKKAL sar-tin sic
	4	[. . . .(.)] i-tu!-ra! (U)
	5	ú-ta-me sic
	6	[^{1}s]i-lim-aš+šur

ADD 168 (AR 651)	Obv 7	ina URU-ana-tú 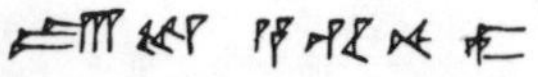 (sic!)
	10	⌜LUGAL!⌝ u DUMU-LUGAL
	Edge 11	[. . . . .]  SUM-an
	Rev 3	[IGI . . . . .]-⌜15!⌝ :
	4	[IGI ^{1}na-b]u!-u-a
	5	IGI ⌜^{1}nu!-uš!-ku!⌝-DINGIR-a-a :
	8	IGI ^{1}e-⌜di⌝-DINGIR
	10	[IGI ^{1}]⌜a!⌝-bu-nu
	L.E. 11	[IGI] ^{1}MAN-PAB
ADD 169 (AR 648)	Rev 1'	IGI ^{1}E[N!-. . . . . .]
	3'	IGI ^{1}I-1[5! . . . .] (U)
	4'	IGI ^{1}SUHUŠ-^{d}PA [. .]!
ADD 171 (AR 646)	Obv 2'	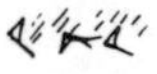 ⌜ša! de!-⌝ni 4 MA.NA KUG.UD
	3'	ša ^{1}PAB-bu-u-
	Edge 7'	i-[GAL]-bi!
	Rev 2	IGI ^{1}U.U!-i
	4	ša URU-ḫu-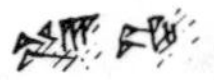
	5	[IGI ^{1}. . . L]Ú*-kala-pu š[i-pi-ri-ti] (U)
	L.E. 1	[. . . . .-e]ri!-ba! (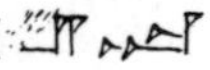)
	2	[. . . L]Ú*!-NIGIR!-E.GAL
ADD 172 (AR 461)	Obv 3	followed by dividing line, unused space for stamp seal impressions, and another dividing line
	4	^{1}PAB-ši-na!(U) LÚ-U.ŠIBIR (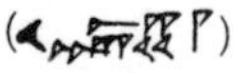) sic
	11	la-qí [tu-a-r]u! de-e-nu DUG$_4$.DUG$_4$
	12	la-áš-š[ú man-nu ša ina ur-kiš] ⌜ina!⌝ ma!-⌜te!⌝-[m]a!
	13	i-zaq-qup-⌜an!⌝-[ni GIL-u-ni]
	14	lu-u ^{1}mu-še-zib-mar-duk [lu-u DUMU-MEŠ-šú]! (U)
	15	lu-u PAB-MEŠ-šu lu-u DUMU-D[UMU!-MEŠ-šú]
	16	ša de-e-nu DUG$_4$.DU[G$_4$ TA*]! (U)
	17	^{1}rém-an-ni-^{d}IM DUM[U-MEŠ-šú]! (U)
	18	ù DUMU-DUMU-MEŠ-šú ub-t[a-u-ni] (U)
	Rev 14	^{1}šum-ma-ta*-še-zib sic
	17	URU-im!-gúr!-^{d}BE (U)
ADD 173 (AR 487)	Obv 2	^{1}la-te!-gi-^{d}na-na-a-a! (U*)
	4	followed by dividing line, three impressions of oval stamp seal, and another dividing line

ADD 173 (AR 487) Obv 12 tu-a-ru de-nu DUG$_{4}$.DUG$_{4}$! la-šú! (U)

13 im-te-ma sic

16 [l]u!-u! DUMU-DUMU-MEŠ-šú-nu [lu]!-⌜u!⌝ PAB-MEŠ-šú-nu (U*)

17 [ša T]A*! ^{1}ri-ba-a-te [DUMU]-MEŠ!-[šú]

Edge and first line of Rev. destroyed

Rev 1'! ina bur-⌜ki⌝ [. . . . .]

6'! IGI ^{1}10-PAB-AŠ [IGI ^{1}].⌜d!⌝PA!-ÁG!-Z[I]

7'! IGI $^{1.d}$MAŠ!-i [O]

8'! IGI $^{1.d}$PA-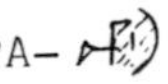 . . . .]

9'! IGI ^{1}DÙG!.[G]A!-GIŠ!.[MI-^{d}.]

10'! IGI $^{1.d}$U+G[UR!-M]AŠ [LÚ]-A.BA

13'! URU-a-li-[ḫi]

ADD 175 (AR 203) Obv 1 ^{1}sa-a-AD sic (thus also Obv.4)

2 EN LÚ* SUM-an-ni sic

——————————!

two stamp seal impressions

——————————!

8 zar!-pu la-qi-[u]! (zar written U$_{8}$)

9 tu-a-ri (sic) de-e-⌜nu!⌝[DUG$_{4}$.DUG$_{4}$ la-áš-šú]

11 i-za-qa-p[a!-ni (sic)

Rev 1 

4 ^{d}15 ⌜a⌝-[ši-bat . .]

7 ^{1}qi!()-ti-DINGIR-MEŠ

10 ^{1}ṣa!-du-⌜ru!⌝

14 ^{1}  -su-nu

Edge 19 LÚ*-SUKKAL LÚ*-2-⌜ú!⌝

ADD 176 (AR 630) Obv 2 ṣu-[pur ^{1}za]-ku!-ri

3 followed by dividing line, 4 fingernail impressions, and another dividing line

6 TA*! IGI! ^{1}za-kù-ri

7 [ina ŠÀ-b]i! (U)

9 [za-ri]p! laq!-qi! tu-a-ru de-⌜e⌝-[nu O!]

10 [DUG$_{4}$].DUG$_{4}$! la!-áš!-šú man-nu ša ina u[r-kiš O!]

11 ina! ma!-te!-ma! i-za-qu-pa-⌜a!⌝-[ni] (U*)

12 [10 MA].NA! KUG!.UD! SUM!-an! LÚ! ⌜ú!⌝-[še-ṣa]

13 [ṣib-tu] be!-en!-nu! ana! 1 me UD-me

14 [s]a!-ar!-tu! ina kàl UD-MEŠ

15 [I]GI! [^{1}]EN!-BÀD! LÚ*!-GAL-URU-MEŠ-ni

16 [IGI] ^{1}!⌜du?⌝()-su-su

ADD 176 (AR 630)	Rev	1	IGI! $^{1!}$m[i]l!-ku-DINGIR
		2	IGI! $^{1!.d!}$UTU!-še-zib
		3	[IGI] $^{1!}$a!-ta-ra
		4	[IGI] $^{1!.d!}$E[N]/M[AŠ]-mu-še-zib
		5	this line does not exist (U)
		9	LÚ*!(not LÚ)-GAR.KUR U[RU]-⌜i⌝-sa-na
		10	[IGI ^{1}]$^{.d}$[A]G!(not PA)-SUM-PAB-MEŠ
		12	2! MA.NA
ADD 177 (AR 183)	Obv	1	^{1}U.GUR-D[U] (U)
		2	URU-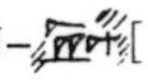[. . .]
		3	followed by dividing line, 3 circular stamp seal impressions, and another dividing line
		4	^{1}[bul]-luṭ-ṭu (U)
		9	[ina 1 M]A.⌜NA⌝-e ša [. .]
	Rev	3	i-šak-kan šú[m!-ma . . .]
		4	⌜a⌝-[d]e-e ša M[AN ina qa-t]i!-šú
		5	[ú-b]a!-'u ITU-[. UD]-20-KÁM
		7	[IGI ^{1}. . .]-⌜i!⌝
		9	[IGI ^{1}. . .]-⌜a!⌝-a
		10	[IGI ^{1}. .]-⌜DINGIR!⌝-a-a
		11	IGI ^{1}šá-ni!-ia LÚ*-A.BA
		12	sic
	Edge	14	A ^{1}EN-GIŠ.TIR(wr. 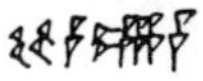, for qīšti ?) [.]
	L.E.	3	[. . . IGI ^{1}ta]r!-di-ia LÚ*!-GIŠ-GIGIR
ADD 179 (AR 473)	Obv	1	ṣu-pur-[šú] (U)
		3	LÚ* SUM-an sic
			————————————!
			four groups of finger-nail impressions
			————————————!
		5	^{1}a-tu-e-ri! (last vertical of -ri very faint)
		6	TA*!(not TA) IGI
		8!	kas-pu ga-mur ta-ad-din (U; Johns omits whole line)
		9!	LÚ* šu-a-ti za-rip laq-qi (U; Johns omits)
		10!	[tu-a]-⌜ru⌝ de-e-ni da-ba-bu
	Rev	1'!	[. . . . . . .]
		3'!	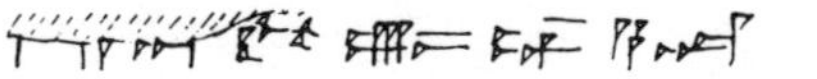
		5'!	^{1}ab-du!-^{d}a-gu-u-ni (U)
		11'!	^{1}at-ta-a'!-⌜ni⌝ (U)

ADD 185 (AR 483)	Obv	2	followed by a dividing line and a cylinder seal impression
	Rev	1	[. MA.NA KUG.G]I! ina! ⌜bur!-ki! $^{d!}$15!⌝ N[INA!-KI]
		2	[i-šak-k]an! kas-pu etc.
		3	[ú-ta]!-ra
		4	[IGI ^{1}]ú-a-ar-bi-is LÚ-3.U$_5$! (no -šú- after 3-!)
		10	IGI ^{1}DINGIR-0!-mu-še-zib
		11	IGI ^{1}⌜dà!⌝-ri-MAN
		13	dan-nat šu-a!-[te]
		15	LÚ-3.U$_5$-šú sic
		16	LÚ-GIŠ-GIGIR! DU$_8$-MEŠ
ADD 188 (AR 479) +ADD 183 (AR 466)	Obv	2	[. . .] ša! LÚ*!-šá!-IGI!-É.GAL
		3	[EN L]Ú! SUM-ni
			cylinder seal impression (dividing lines above and below!)
		4	$^{1.d}$PA-EN-PAB L[Ú*]!-NINDA! ÌR-šú
		8	1 MA.NA KUG.UD ina URU-gar-⌜gar!⌝-[mis]
		15	[ša]! TA*!(not TA) ^{1}rém-a-ni-10
	Rev	1	[ù]! DUMU-MEŠ-š[ú de-n]u! DUG$_4$.DUG$_4$
		3	DUG$_4$.DUG$_4$-[ma]
		4	bé-nu sic (U: be-)
		6	I[GI ^{1}.] [. . . .]
		7	destroyed
		8	[. . . . . .] [. .] (= ADD 188 r1')
		9	[. . . . . .] [. .]
		10	[. . . . .] ⌜LÚ*!-GAL!-ki!⌝-[ṣir]! (= ADD 188 r2')
		11	[IGI $^{1.d}$. .]-⌜ú!⌝-pa-ḫír!
			4 lines blank
		12	[ITU-. UD]-21-KÁM
		14	[IGI ^{1}a]-ḫi!-ṭa!-ba
		15	[IGI $^{1.d}$PA]!-SUM-PAB-MEŠ
ADD 197 (AR 488)	Obv	1	^{1}10-ra-⌜pa!⌝-a (U)
		2	LÚ-ši-me! (U)
			two stamp seal impressions (dividing lines above and below!)
		6	[il-q]i
	Rev	1'	[. . .] [. .]

ADD 198 (AR 472) Obv 2 followed by dividing line, unused space for stamp seal impressions, and another dividing line

6 il-[qi]!

11 man-n[u ša]! ina u[r]-kiš

12 ina ma-te-e!-ma (U)

15 [lu-u DUMU]!-DUMU!-MEŠ-⌜šu!⌝

16 [ša de-e-nu] ⌜DUG$_4$.DUG$_4$⌝ O!

Rev 1' [ina b]ur-ki [. . . . .] (U)

2' O! NINA-KI GAR-[an . . .]

3' kas-pu O! a-na [10-MEŠ-t]e!

4' ⌜a-na EN⌝-[M]EŠ GUR.RA

5' IGI ^{1}a-[.]-⌜'u!⌝-u

6' IGI ^{1}[. . .]-⌜i!⌝

7' IGI ^{1}⌜na!⌝-zi-[. .] (U)

8' IGI ^{1}nu-nu-a [. .]! (U)

10' IGI $^{1.d}$PA-MU- [L]Ú-A.BA

ADD 200 (AR 482) Obv 2 followed by dividing line, cylinder seal impression, and another dividing line

5 ^{1}rém-a-na-^{d}IM sic

8 [ina ŠÀ . M]A!.NA

9 [kas-pu gam-mur t]a!-din L[Ú! š]u!-a!-tu! (U)

10! [za-rip laq-qi tu-a]-ru [. . . .] (U)

Johns' line "11" does not exist

Rev 1 [. . . . . KUG].GI!

2 [ina bur-ki ^{d}]iš-tar sic (U incorrectly [ša ^{d}])

3 ⌜a⌝-ši-⌜bat URU-NINA-KI⌝ GAR-an

7 $^{1.d}$šá-maš-[šal]!-lim LÚ*-[.]! ša É.GAL

8 IGI ^{1} [. .] LÚ*-A.⌜ZU!⌝ (^{1}⌜ba⌝-n[i-i] possible)

9 IGI ^{1}⌜ṣil!⌝-la-a (U)

10 ša O! GAL-u-rat-MEŠ (U)

ADD 201 (AR 38) Obv 2 followed by dividing lines, unused space for stamp seal impressions, and another dividing line

6 TA*! (not TA) IGI ^{1}zu-un-b[i]

11 [t]u!-a!-ru (U*)

12 [. .]! 1 me UD-me! [. . . . .] (break)

Rev 1 [IGI ^{1}. .] ba! [. . .]

2 [IGI ^{1}. .]-nu [. . .]!

3 [IGI ^{1}. .]x [. . .]!

ADD 201 (AR 38) Rev 4 [IGI 1. . . .]x [. . . .]!
5 [IGI 1. . . A]Š! [. . .]!
6 [IGI 1. . .] [. .]!
7 [IGI 1. . .] ni [.]!
8 [IGI] 1!.d!iš!-tar!-ba!-[.]!
blank space of about 3 lines
9 ITU-DUL sic

ADD 204 (AR 481) Obv 2 followed by dividing line, unused space for stamp
seal impressions, and another dividing lin
4 1.dPA-u-⌜a!⌝ [LÚ-m]an-za-si! ⌜x⌝-te! (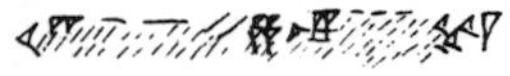)
Rev 1' IGI 1man-nu-ki-⌜NINA!-KI!⌝ ⌜LÚ⌝-šá-IGI-[. .]
4' 1suk-ku-a-a sic

ADD 206 (AR 196) Obv 2 EN LÚ SUM-an!-[ni]
———————————————!
two impressions of square stamp seal
———————————————!
3 [1. . . -AP]IN-eš
4 [. . . . . .] mal!() lu
5 [. . . . GAR|.KUR!(sup.ras.)-tu
6 [. . . . U]RU!-aš+šur (cf. r2)
7 [ina ŠÀ . GÍN-M]EŠ! KUG.UD
15 [lu-u DUMU-DUMU-MEŠ-šú] lu-u PAB-MEŠ-MEŠ!
16 [lu-u mim-ma]-ni!-šú
17 [ša TA* . . . . . .]
Rev 1 MA.N]A
2 [ina bur-ki d.] a-šib!-bi
4 [a-na EN-šú GUR.R]A! ina
6 [DI.KUD de-en-š]ú! la i-šá!-mu-[u]! (no dividing line)
7 [ITU-. UD-.-KAM!] lim-mu 1EN-KASKAL-KUR-u (sic)
8 [IGI 1. . . .] IGI 1.dŠÚ!-ZU!
11 [IGI 1gab-b]u!-DINGIR-MEŠ
12 [IGI 1ba-la]!-si-i
13 [IGI 1.dM]AŠ!-AŠ-A IGI 1EN-⌜lu!⌝-TI
14 [IGI 1. . .]AŠ!-MAN!-DÙ
15 [IGI O! 1] ⌜ITU⌝-AB-a-a
16 [IGI 1. .] -MAŠ
17 IGI 1m[an!-nu]-ki!-NINA-KI (U*)
18 IGI 1ḫa-⌜di⌝-i' IGI 1⌜ú!⌝-[. .] (U)
20 IGI 1g/z[i!-. . .]

ADD 208 (AR 40) Obv 1 ^{1}man-nu-ki-URU-a[rba!-ìl]

2 ta-⌜da⌝-[ni]

——————————————!

3 stamp seal impressions

——————————————!

3 ^{MÍ}bi-li-lu!-tu

6 ina ŠÀ O! ½! MA.NA (U)

7 TA* IGI O! ^{1}man-nu-ki-URU-arba-ìl ta-a[l-qí]

16 a-šib URU-[kal-ḫi] (U)

17 (blank!) GAR-an

Rev 2 GUR.RA [ina la] de-[ni-šú]

7 IGI ^{1}la-[. . . . .]⌜x!⌝ LÚ*-ẋ[. .]

10 IGI ^{1}[. . . . .]-DINGIR!

11! IGI ^{1}[. . . . . .] (omitted by Johns)

12!=Johns "11": at end ^{d}PA now entirely gone

13! IGI $^{1.d!}$[. . . .] (Johns' -iq-bi at end of line now entirely lost)

16 ^{1}ki-ṣir-aš+šur!

17 IGI $^{1.d}$PA-u+a!-a! LÚ*-A.BA

Edge18 ITU-NE UD-27-KAM* lim!-mu! (U)

19 ^{1}mar-la-rim LÚ*-tur-tan URU!-ku-[mu-ḫi]

L.E. 1 ^{1}aš+šur-DÙ-DUMU!+UŠ! (not A!)

ADD 209 (AR 521) Obv 2 [É ^{1}3]0?-MAŠ ḫa-za-[nu] (3)0 = )

3 followed by dividing line, 3 stamp seal impressions, and another dividing line

4 ^{MÍ}AD-li-iḫ-ia sic

12 man-nu ša! [ina ur-kiš] (U)

16 DUG$_4$.DUG$_4$ T[A*! ^{MÍ}GAR.KUR-tú]

Rev 4 kas-pi (sic) a-di 10-MEŠ a-n[a EN-šú GUR.RA]

5 ina de-ni-šú i-DUG$_4$.[DUG$_4$-ma la TI]

one line blank, no dividing line!

8 ^{1}IM-^{d}⌜15!⌝ [. .]

9 $^{1.d}$PA-SIG$_5$-DINGIR!-[MEŠ]

13 ^{1}ḫa-an-nu!()-u-si

14 ^{1}10-na!-ta-an (U)

15 ^{1}[n]a!-ma-ri-MAN!

16 ^{1}[.]!-na-si-i'

On left edge, impression of oval stamp seal (different from that impressed on Obverse)

ADD 210 (AR 204) Obv 2 [LÚ]-SANGA šá ^{d}+E[N? . . . .] (E[N] =)
3 followed by cylinder seal impression; no rulings
4 [^{MÍ}].$^{⌜d⌝}$na-na-a-a-da-[. .] sic
5 ⌜A⌝.MÍ (sic) ^{1}su-qa-a-a ⌜GÉME!⌝-[šú]!
7 ^{1}EN( )-DINGIR-MEŠ- ⌜DUMU!⌝[. .]
8 ^{1}⌜ka!-ku!⌝-la-ni ina ŠÀ-bi
Rev 1 ⌜i!⌝-GIL-u-ni (U)
2 lu DUMU-MEŠ-šú lu ŠEŠ!-MEŠ-[šú]
3 TA* ^{1}BE!-⌜ma!⌝-x[. .] ( )
6 sic
7 [UR]U-ḫi-ra-na sic
8 [a-n]a 10-MEŠ-te
12 ^{1}EN-[KASKAL]-PAB-PAB
13 ^{1}GIN-NU[MUN] possible
14 ^{1}⌜DÙG+GA-IGI⌝-[. .] sic
16 PAB URU-ḫi-ra-[na . . . .]!
Edge19 IGI ^{1}qi-[. . .]
L.E. 1 ^{1}ḫa-am!-GIŠ![. . . . .]-i (sic, not ḫa-bil [U])
2 ^{1}[illegible]-^{d} [A [illegible]
3 PAB URU-[di]-qu-qi-na-a-⌜a!⌝[. . . .] -PAB-MEŠ

ADD 211 (AR 217) Obv 3 ^{1}bu-da-⌜nu!-še!⌝
4 followed by dividing lines, 2 [+1] stamp seal impressions, and another dividing line
5 G[EMÉ]-šú-nu
Rev 2 mim+ma-mu-nu-šu-nu sic
12 [IGI ^{1}k]i-ṣir-aš+šur

ADD 212 (AR 459) Obv 1 [NA_4-KIŠIB]! $^{1.d}$PA-NUMU[N!-AŠ] (U)
2 [EN M]Í ta-da-⌜a!⌝-[ni]
———————————!
3 impressions of circular stamp seal
———————————!
7 [i]l!-qi
8 MÍ šu-a-te za-r[i!-ip]
9 laq-qi (sic) tu-a-⌜ru⌝ d[e-e-nu]
10 DUG_4.DUG_4 la-áš-[šu]
15 [T]A*! ^{1}šum-ma-DINGIR-MEŠ (U)
16 [T]A*! DUMU-⌜MEŠ⌝-šú TA*! DUMU-DU[MU-MEŠ-šú] (U*)
17 [TA*! PA]B!-MEŠ-šú TA*!(not TA) DUMU!-P[AB!-MES-šú] (U*)
Rev 1 [ša d]e!-e-nu DUG_4.DUG_4 (U)

ADD 212 (AR 459) Rev 2 [ub]-ta-'u-O!-ni (U)
5 la laq-qi sic
6 [ṣib]-tu be-en-n[u]! ⸢ina!⸣ 1 me UD-me
7 [s]a!-ar-⸢tú⸣[ina]! kal UD-me

---

8 [IGI ^{1}]$^{.d}$za-b[a$_4$]-⸢ba$_4$⸣-[P]AB-P[A]B
10 IGI ^{1}[.]-DINGIR! LÚ*!-⸢šá!⸣ -
14 [IGI ^{1}. .]-na-DINGIR LÚ*-TIN
15 [IGI ^{1}. .] -a-bu
16 [IGI ^{1}. . . .] [. . .]
L.E. 1 [. . . . . MU]-25!-[KAM] ⸢1!⸣$^{.d}$30-P[AB-MEŠ-SU]
2 (blank) [MAN! KUR] aš+šur-K[I]

ADD 213 (AR 189) Obv 2 followed by dividing line, unused space for stamp seal impressions, and another dividing line
3 $^{MÍ.d}$na-na-TUKU-
7 MÍ šu-[a-te zar-pat]
8 [la]-⸢qi⸣-at man-nu š[a i-za-qu-pa-ni GIL-u-ni]!
9! [lu-u ^{1}dà]-ri!-AD!-[u-a lu-u DUMU-MEŠ-šú] (U)
10! [lu-u DUMU-DUMU-MEŠ-šú l]u!-u [ŠEŠ-MEŠ-šú]
11! [lu-u DUMU-PAB-MEŠ-šú šá TA*]!

ADD 214 (AR 510) Obv 1'! [. . . . . .] [. . . . . .]

---!

two [+1] impressions of large stamp seal with Aramaic seal legend

---!

4'! [L]Ú-SAG LUGAL ina ŠÀ-bi 35! GÍN-MEŠ
10'! ⸢i⸣-za-qu-O!-ni GIL-u-ni
Rev 1 ina bur-ki ina! bur!-k[i! . . . . .(.)] (sic, cf. Obv.8')
10 LÚ-mu-kil-ap!-MEŠ (U)
12 [IGI ^{1}DINGIR]-im-me! DAM.QA[R]

ADD 215 (AR 166) Obv 2 followed by dividing line, 2 [+1] impressions of circular stamp seal, and another dividing line
3 [^{MÍ}]^{1}AD-ḫa-'a-li [GEMÉ-šú]!
4 ša ^{1}se-e'-za-b[a-di]!
5 ú-piš-ma ^{MÍ}la-te-gi!-⸢a!⸣-[na-. .]
6 TA*!(not TA)
9 MÍ šu-a-⸢tu⸣ zar-[pa]t ⸢laq!-qi!⸣-at
11 ur-kiš u! ma-[te-m]e! (U)
Rev 1 ⸢2⸣ or ⸢5⸣ [M]A.NA KUG.UD

ADD 215 (AR 166)	Rev 7	^{1}ḫa-an-di-i LÚ-na!-ši-i
	9	IGI ^{1}[ḫ]a!-⌜su!⌝-si-i
	10	[IGI ^{1}. .]-AŠ!-A LÚ-⌜NIGÍR!⌝
	11	[IGI ^{1}. . . ḫ]a-ṣab!-⌜ḫu⌝-n[i]!
ADD 216 (AR 517)	Obv 1'	[LÚ*-SAN]GA! ⌜ša⌝ ^{d}⌜EN⌝
	4'	i-⌜si!-qi⌝ :! kas-pu
	5'	za-rip la-qi O! (following la-qi, on edge, faint traces reading 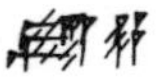, probably erased tu-a-; cf. line 6')
	6'	tu()-a-ru DI.KUD O! DUG$_4$.DUG$_4$ la-⌜áš⌝-[šú] (U*)
	7'	ša BAL-kàt-tu!-u-ni (U)
	8'	O! 1 MA.NA KUG.UD 1! MA!.NA! KUG!.G[I]!
	9'	ina [.] ša URU-ni-nu-[a]
	Rev 1	kas-pu ina 10-M[EŠ-te
	3	sic
	7	[LÚ*-ṣa-ri]p!-KUŠ-DUḪ.ŠI.A
	8	[. . .][. . .]
	L.E. 2	(blank) LÚ*!-[. . . .]
ADD 217 (AR 518)	Obv	Beginning lost
		three oval stamp seal impressions
	1'	[^{MI}.]-di-bé!-e-šá-ŠÀ-bi (U)
	3'	^{1}ṣal-mu-PAB-MEŠ [O]!
	10'	G[IL!-u-ni] (U)
	11'	TA*!(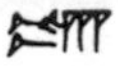) ^{1}ṣal-mu-PAB-M[EŠ! DUMU-MEŠ-šú]
	12'	[DUMU]-⌜DUMU⌝-MEŠ-š[ú ub-ta-u-ni]
ADD 218 (AR 188)	Obv 4'	man-nu ša ina ur-kiš lu-u ina! ⌜ma!-ti!-ma!⌝ (U*)
	5'	i-za-qu-ba!-ni (U)
	7'	1 MA.NA KUG.UD SUM-an i!-paṭ!-ṭar!
	8'	O! ITU-ŠU UD-15!-KÁM (U*)
	Rev 1	^{1}man-nu-GIM-10 GAL-[. .]! (U)
	2	sic
	8	IGI ^{1}[du]-un!-qí-15 [O?]
	9	[IGI ^{1}. . .]-⌜a⌝-a [. .]
ADD 219 (AR 519)	Obv 1'	[. . . . .]-AŠ O!
	2'	[ina ŠÀ-bi]! 1! ½ KUG.UD TA*! IGI!-šu!-nu! (U*)

ADD 219 (AR 519) Obv 3' [il-qi! kas-pu] gam-mur (U)
4' [šu-a-tu! za-ár-pa]t! la-qí-at (U*)
Edge 10' [GUR.RA ina la] de-ni-šú
11! [DUG_4.DUG_4-ma la TI-q]í!
Rev 1 [. . . . .
2 [. . . . .] É!-MEŠ!
3 [IGI ^{1}gi/ḫa-r]i!-U.U!
4 [IGI $^{1.d}$]PA+TÚG!-AŠ (U)
6 [IGI ^{1}. .-b]i!-a-tar!
7 [IGI ^{1}. .]-di-i LÚ*-mu-kil-KUŠ-PA!-MEŠ (U)
8 [IGI ^{1}. .]-a!-nu-MAN LÚ*-3!-šú!

ADD 221 (AR 503) Obv Beginning lost
————————————!
[n+]1 stamp seal impression[s]
————————————!
1' ^{MÍ}šam!-s[i!-. .] GEMÉ!-šú! (U*)
2' DUMU ⸢GA!⸣ [.(.).]-MEŠ
3' ú-piš-ma ^{1}[.(.)] -a-a
4' ŠÀ-⸢bi⸣ [. MA.NA] ⸢KUG⸣.UD-MEŠ!
5' il-qi ⸢kas-pu⸣ g[a]-⸢mur⸣
6' ta-din ⸢MÍ DUMU⸣ [šu]-a-te
7' za-ar-pu la[q-qi]!-iu!-u!
Edge destroyed
Rev 1 [man-nu ša]! ⸢de!⸣-e!-nu ⸢DUG_4!.DUG_4!⸣ [0]
2 ⸢ub!-ta!-u!-ni!⸣ KUG!.UD! [a-n]a!
3 10!-MEŠ!-⸢te! a!-na!⸣ EN-MEŠ-[šú] GUR
————————————!
4 I[GI! ^{1}]-⸢x x x x⸣
5 I[GI!] $^{1!.⸢d!⸣}$
6 IGI! $^{1!}$[.]-MAN!-DÙ!
7 IGI! $^{1!}$[. . .]-a-nu ⸢x x⸣
balance destroyed
L.E. 1 [IGI ^{1}.(.)]x-me IGI ^{1}ṣa-la-a-a $^{1!}$[. . .]
2 [lim-mu]! ^{1}U.U!-i LÚ*-IGI+UM IGI [. . . .]

ADD 228 (AR 641) Obv 4' URU-ana-na! GAR (U; sic)
Rev 1 ^{1}ku-ru-ku EN-ŠU+2-MEŠ ša!(not šá) MÍ
2 ^{1}iš-ta-AN-BU sic
6 [IGI ^{1}]$^{.⸢d!⸣}$PA-[za]!-qip-SIG

ADD 229 (AR 64) Obv 2 followed by dividing line, two circular stamp

ADD 229 (AR 64) seal impressions, and another dividing line
9 ^{1}se-ma-a-di sic
Rev 3 followed by dividing line (!)
4 LÚ*-tam-QAR sic
7 ^{1}ku!-i-sa-a
10 ITU-DUL sic

ADD 230 (AR 60) Obv 2 followed by dividing line, cylinder seal impression, and another dividing line
6 TA*!(not TA) IGI $^{1.d}$AG!(not PA)-SU
7 6! MA.NA (U)
Rev 2 wr. LÚ-(space) 3.(space) U_5
3 IGI ^{1}DI!-mu!-EN!-la!-mur! KI+MIN (U)
5 IGI ^{1}man!-nu!-ki!-$^{d!}$15!-ZU! LÚ!-KI+MIN (U)
7 ^{1}U.U!-DÙ
9 IGI ^{1}ku!-si-si-i IGI $^{1.d}$MAŠ!-i (U)
12 LÚ-A.BA ṣa-bit e-gir-te! (U)

ADD 231 (AR 202) Obv 2 followed by dividing line, two stamp seal impressions, and another dividing line
4 ^{1}DINGIR-su!-ri O! ŠEŠ-MEŠ-šú (U)
9 ina šá O! gar-ga-miš (U)
10 ta(wr. )-din
Edge 15 ub-ta-u-[ni]
Rev 6 la i-la!-qi (U)
———————————!
7 IGI ^{1}10-ta-ka-a sic
10 IGI ^{1}se-e'-ḫu-ut-ni LÚ*-GIŠ!.GIGIR!
11 $^{1.d}$PA-I sic
12 IGI ^{1}blank!
3 lines blank; date

ADD 232 (AR 458) Obv 2 followed by dividing line, cylinder seal impression, and another dividing line
3 ^{1}IM-4-i ÌR [. . . .]-IM-AN.ŠÁR
4 $^{MÍ.d}$ur-kit-DINGIR-a-a [. . . .]!
5 É PAB 5 ZI-MEŠ
Rev 1 man-nu šá TA*! (not TA)
8 ^{1}10!-KI-ia
10 ^{1}MAN-SIPA(wr. 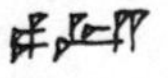)-u+a!
13 ^{1}e-zi-pa-⌜šar!⌝

ADD 233 (AR 208)	Obv 2	NA$_4$-KIŠIB ^{1} . . .]
	3	DUMU ^{1}ḫa-zi-[. . . . .] (U)
	4	EN MÍ-[MEŠ SUM-ni] (U)
		——————————!
		two oval stamp seal impressions
		——————————!
	5	^{MÍ}ḫa-am-bu-su GE[MÉ-šú-n]u!
	6	ina UGU [. .]
	9	MA.⌜NA⌝ 8 GÍN KUG!.UD! (U)
	12	zar$_4$-pat- la-qi-'a
	Rev 2	ša TA*! (not TA)
	16	sic (-ri written)
ADD 235 (AR 231)	Obv 2	followed by dividing lines, three stamp seal impressions, and another dividing line
	Rev 7	KUR!( )-e sic (U incorrectly MAN.E)
	8	a-na ^{1}kak-kul-la-ni S[UM!-an]
	15	^{1}ḫu-ba-⌜šá!⌝-a-te (U)
ADD 236 (AR 80)	Obv 1	ṣu-pur ^{1}ki-qi-la!-ni L[Ú*-. .]
	2	followed by dividing line, 6 finger-nail impressions, and another dividing line
	4	[PAB 2 LÚ*!]-ÌR-MEŠ ša ^{1}ki-qi-⌜la!⌝-ni!
	8	^{1}ki-qi-la!-ni
	14	[ina b]ur-ki ^{d}NIN.[LÍL]
ADD 237 (AR 71)	Obv 2	followed by dividing line, three oval stamp seal impresssions, and another dividing line
	5	LÚ-mu!-kil!-KUŠ-PA-MEŠ (U)
	7	ta-din! (U)
	13	TA* ^{1}rém-an-ni- ^{d}IM ⌜ù!⌝ [. . .] (U)
	Rev 2	ina bur-ki ^{d}⌜GAŠAN!-NINA!⌝-[KI GAR-an]
	3	kas-pi (sic) a-na 10-MEŠ-te a-n[a! . . . . .]
	5	LÚ-EN.N[AM! . . .]
	7	$^{1.d}$U+GUR!-LUGAL-PAB
	8	IGI ^{1}ki-ṣir-aš+šur! LÚ!-ḫa!-za!-nu! (U)
	9	IGI ^{1}al!-DINGIR-mil-ki
	11	^{1}ri-ḫi-me-MAN sic (but cf. ADD 352 r4'!)
	12	DUMU $^{1.}$⌜$^{d!}$+EN⌝-A-SUM-na
	13	IGI $^{1.d}$IM-ša[l-l]im DUMU ^{1}a-⌜šir!⌝( )-a
	14	(end) ^{1}ba!-ri-ki!

ADD 238 (AR 201)	Obv 2	[ṣu-pur ^{1}EN-KASKAL-K]I-ia etc.
		2 [+1] fingernail impressions (in horizontal position) !
	4	[^{1} . . .] 
	6	PAB 15 [ZI-MEŠ Ì]R-MEŠ ša ^{1}EN-KAS[KAL-K]I!-[i]a
	7	^{1}šum-ma-DI[NGIR]-ME[Š]!
	8	LÚ*-mu-kil-⸢PA⸣-[M]EŠ!
	Edge! 20	O! DUMU-MEŠ-šú ù DUMU-DUMU!-MEŠ-šú (U)
	Rev 9	^{1}da!(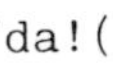)-lu!-u-a LÚ*-A.ZU (U)
	14	[š]a! LÚ*-G[AL]!-K[A]!.KEŠDA
	15	[IGI ^{1}]⸢za⸣-a!-zi-i [LÚ*-m]u-DIB-P[A-MEŠ]
	16	ša LÚ*-KA[Š.LUL] (U)
	18	^{1}SUM-PAB-MEŠ LÚ*-G[AR!.KUR (U)
ADD 240 (AR 59)	Obv 3	followed by a dividing line, 2 [+n] fingernail impressions (in vertical position), and another dividing line
	10	⸢ina!⸣ MA.NA ša UR[U-
	Edge 15	tu-a-ru [de-e-nu DUG$_4$.DUG$_4$ la lú šú!]
	Rev 1	[man-n]u! š[a! i-za-qu-pa-an-ni]
	2	[. MA].NA! K[UG!.UD i-dan]
	6	$^{1.d}$U.GUR-MU!-[DÙ] sic (U: -NUMUN-)
	9	LÚ*-⸢šá!⸣-[. . .]
	13	^{1}pa-[q]a!-ḫ[a! LÚ-GAL-URU-MEŠ]
	18	LÚ*-GAR.KUR [. . .]
ADD 241 (AR 73)	Obv 2	followed by dividing line, cylinder seal impression, and another dividing line
	3	(end) DUMU.MÍ!-[su]
	4	[PAB 4 $^{1.d}$]⸢PA!⸣-[. . . .(.)] DUMU-MEŠ-šú DUMU.MI 2 ⸢MU⸣[..]
	5	PAB 7! ^{1}GIŠ.MI-E[N . .]⸢x x⸣ šú! [. . .] (U*)
	6	(end) PAB-[šú PAB 3]!
	7	(end) ⸢^{1}⸣[I-DING]IR
	8	TA*!(not TA) IGI
	15	i-GIL-[ú]!-ni (spaced out)
	Rev 3	$^{1.d}$PA-⸢ka!⸣-in-MAN! LÚ*-⸢GAL!⸣-[. . .]
	4	^{1}ḫal-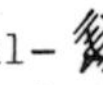 -pa!-a-a (U)
	5	IGI ^{1}⸢ba!-du$_8$!⸣-du$_8$! LÚ*-: (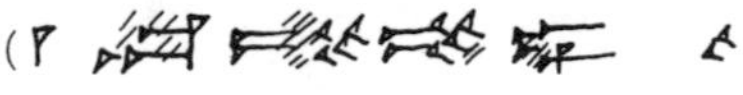)
	6	^{1}ITU-⸢AB!⸣-a-a

Rev 7 ^{1}ḫal-[d]i!-ŠE[Š]!-PAB (sic) LÚ*-mu!-GUR!-UMUŠ
9 ^{1}SUḪU[Š!-. .] LÚ*-Ì.DU$_{8}$
10 LÚ*]-⸢ḫa-za⸣-nu ⸢ša!⸣ URU-qu-da!-ru! (U*)
11 $^{1.d}$3[0!-TI-s]u-⸢E LÚ*⸣-[.]
(blank space of about 7 lines)

ADD 242 (AR 457) Obv 2 ^{1}ki-qil-⸢la!⸣-[nu]
3 followed by dividing line, unused(!) space for stamp seal impressions, and another dividing line
8 ina 1 MA-e (sic!) šá MAN
12 la-qi!(not qí)-u (U)
15 [i-za-qu-pa-n]i ⸢4!⸣ MA.NA
16 KUG].GI
Rev 2 kas-p[u a-na 10]-MEŠ-te
3 be-en sic
5 UD-me! (U)
11 $^{1.d}$⸢PA!⸣(not AG)-MAŠ
two lines blank before date

ADD 243 (AR 207) Obv 3 followed by dividing line, cylinder seal impression(!), and another dividing line
3 L[Ú-
5 ^{MÍ}re-mu-t[ú sic (U:-bu-)
9 TA*!(not TA) IGI
11 il-qi!(not -qí) (U)
Edge! 15! la-áš-šú! man-nù! ša! ur-kiš! (U*)
Rev 1 [ina ma-te-ma i-za-q]u-pa-ni
3 [. . . . . . lu-u mim-m]a!-ni-šú
14 sic
Edge 20 lim-mu ^{1}id-di[n]-[illegible][. .]

ADD 244 (AR 159) Obv 14 1 MA.NA 0! SÍG-qer-du KÚ! (U)
16 ina bur-ki ^{d}I[M]!
17 GAR-[an]! (U)
19 DUG$_{4}$.DUG$_{4}$-ma! la [i-laq-qi]! (U)
Rev 4 IGI ^{1}[illegible]⸢LÚ*⸣-[SAG]
9 LÚ*-NAGAR!

ADD 245 (AR 81) Obv 2 E[N] M[Í][illegible]S[UM-ni]
———————————— !
cylinder seal impression
———————————— !

Obv 4 sic
Rev 4 ^{d}15 a-šib! NINA-KI (U; sic)
9 ^{1}mil-ki-la!-[rim]
10 ^{1}URU!()-ú-[. . .] (cf. 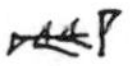 = ba in Rev.1)
11 followed by a break of about two lines

ADD 246 (AR 82) Obv 1 [. . . . .]!
3! [NA$_4$-KIŠIB] ^{1}a-- mu-ia
4! [PA]B! A ^{1}EN-KASKAL-tak-lak (U)
5! indented
3 stamp seal impressions, no ruling
6! ^{1}ŠEŠ-nu-ri DAM!-šú (U) DUMU.MÍ-šú (sic) PAB 3
7! ⌜3!⌝ DUMU-MEŠ (U)
10! ^{1}šúm-mu!-DINGIR-MEŠ sic (U: -ma-)
12! i-za-rip sic
Rev 1 la-a-ši sic
2 LÚ*!(not LÚ)-EN.NAM
5 GIL written 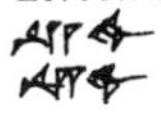
6 1 MA.NA ⌜KUG.GI!⌝
8 LÚ*!(not LÚ) 2 i ša UŠ!-kib!-šú ()
9 IGI ^{1}i-la-a (sic) ša LÚ*!-GÌR?+2 ()
10 sic
13 ^{1}AD-i-qa-mu! sic (U: -ma)
14 [IG]I ^{1}30-za-qi!-pi (U)
15 [IGI ^{1}]EN!-DÙ (U)
16 [IGI ^{1}]DI!-mu-ŠEŠ-MEŠ ša ḫu-ṭa-ru!
17 [IGI ^{1}. . . LÚ!-ÌR ša DUMU-MAN

ADD 248 (AR 455) Obv Beginning destroyed; then blank space with stamp seal impression
______________________________!
9 ⌜la!⌝-[q]i-⌜ú⌝ sic (U: -la[q-)
Rev 3 LÚ*-E[N.NAM] URU-šú
5 a-na EN-šú! ⌜ú⌝-t[a-ra] (U)
7 be-⌜en-nu⌝ [ṣib]!-tu! a-na 1 me UD-me
10 ^{1}DINGIR-ma-LID-BAN! LÚ*-GÍR.LÁ (sic!)
13! IGI ^{1}aš+šur!-AŠ! DUMU! 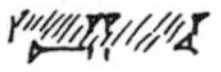 (U; Johns omits whole line)
16! [. . . . . L]Ú*!-ma-k[i!-su]

ADD 252 (AR 633) Obv Beginning destroyed, then 2 stamp seal impressions followed by a dividing line

2 [PAB]! 3 ÌR-MEŠ ⌜DUMU!⌝-DUMU-MEŠ

3 ⌜LÚ*⌝-GAL-ki-ṣir ša LU[GAL]! (U)

4 [ina Š]À-bi (U)

5 [kas]!-pu gam-mur ... zar$_4$-pu laq!-⌜qí!⌝-[u] (U)

7 [man-n]u

8 URU-sa-mar-na!

11 [de-e-nu] ⌜DUG$_4$!.DUG$_4$!⌝ i-gar-ru-u-ni

12 (= Edge) destroyed

Rev 1 [. . . . .]

2 [. . . . .] ⌜x x x x x x⌝ [. .]

3! [kas-pu a-na] 10-MEŠ-te [a-na] EN-MEŠ-⌜šú⌝ GUR.R[A]!

4! [ina de-ni-šú DUG$_4$.DUG$_4$-m]a! la il!()-⌜laq⌝-[qi]

————————————————————————————— !

5-11 unreadable

12 [IGI ^{1}]⌜a⌝-zi-i [. . . . .]

ADD 255 (AR 50) Obv 2 followed by impression of a cylinder seal; no rulings

4 [^{1}]si-ti-ir-ka-a-nu

5 [g]ab-bu

8 ina ŠÀ-bi [. . . . . . .]

9 [TA* I]GI

Rev 3' ^{1}KÁ-ti!-nu-ra-a-a ( ...)

4' LÚ*-SANGA šá! (not ša)

5' LÚ*-SANGA šá! (U)

6' šá! (U)

7' ša (sic) ^{d}GAŠAN!-KUR-ḫa (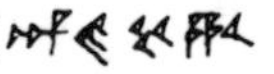)

16' ^{1}NUNUZ-a-a A!.BA! [. . .] (U)

17' ITU-DIRI!.ŠE UD-14-KAM lim-mu ^{1}[Manzarnê]

18' LÚ*-GAR.KUR URU-ku!-l[a-ni-a]

ADD 253 (AR 85) Obv Beginning destroyed; then space for seal impressions (no impressions extant)

————————————————————————————— !

1' [. . .]-LÚ-lu-šá-⌜lim!⌝-šú 1! DUMU G[A]!

2' [. . . M]Í-šú

3' [^{1}. . .] 2 MÍ-MEŠ-šú

5' [. . . U]N-MEŠ šá ^{1}SUḪUŠ-^{d}

11' tu-a-r]u de-e-nu

12' now completely destroyed

ADD 253 (AR 85) Rev 1' [IGI ^{1}. . . . LÚ]-⸢A!.BA!⸣ ša DUMU-MAN
2' [IGI ^{1}. . . . L]Ú-GAL-kal!-lap! (U)
3' [IGI ^{1}. . . . ^{1}]!AN.ŠÁR-EN-PAB LÚ-GAR.KUR (U)
4' [IGI ^{1}. . . . ^{1}]$^{⸢d⸣}$PA-⸢PAB⸣-[SUM]-na
5' [(blank!)] LÚ-mu-tar-UMUŠ-MEŠ!
7' beginning of line left blank
9' [IGI ^{1}z]i!-zi-i LÚ-mu-tar-UMUŠ-[M]EŠ!
10' [. . . .]  -MEŠ la maḫ-ru-u!-[ti]!

ADD 254 (AR 192) Obv Beginning destroyed; then seal space with 2[+1] impressions of stamp seal
————————————————————!
4' TA*! IGI
7' ina 1 MA.NA-e 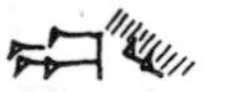 . . .]
Edge 10' là-TI sic
Rev 7 IGI $^{1.⸢d!}$PA!⸣-TÉŠ-ka-ZI

ADD 256 (AR 536) Obv 3 followed by a dividing line, impression of a cylinder seal, and another dividing line
11 [. . il-q]i kas-pu 0!
12 [gam-mur! ta-din] MÍ-MEŠ
Rev 5' [IGI ^{1}. . .]-a'! LÚ*!-DAM.QAR (U)
6' LÚ*-GIGIR ša! nu!-rat ()
8' IGI ^{1}ḫa-làḫ-[a-a . .]
one line blank
9' IGI ^{1}mar-du-u-a L[Ú*-A.BA]!
two lines blank; date

ADD 257 (AR 66) Obv 1 [NA$_{4}$]- KIŠIB! ^{1}[^{d}P]A-[EN-PAB] (name virtually lost)
————————————————————!
unused space for stamp seal impressions
————————————————————!
2 looks like ^{MÍ}⸢mar⸣-[ṭ]a!-ḫi-⸢ia!⸣ GEMÉ⸣-[šú . . .]
(), despite Aram. 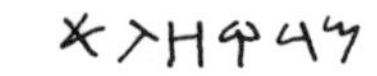 in r10f
4 ú-[piš]-⸢ma⸣ ^{1}[^{d}PA]-u-[a]
5 TA* pa-an ^{1}[^{d}PA?]-⸢EN⸣-[PAB]
6 ina ŠÀ 2 MA.NA KUG.UD ina! 1! M[A.NA] (U*)
8 (end) ga-m[ur ta-din]!
9 ⸢É!⸣ M[Í-MEŠ šu]-⸢a⸣-t[ú] za-ar-p[u! la-qi-u]!
12 [i-za-qu-p]a!-a!-[ni] (U*)
3 lines destroyed
Edge 2 lines in Aramaic

ADD 257 (AR 66) Rev 1 [ša! TA*] $^{1.d}$PA-u-a
2 [DUMU-DUMU-M]EŠ!-šú
3 [ub-t]a-O!-u-ni 5! MA.NA K[UG.UD LUḪ-u] (U)
7 a-na DÙ.A! /// [. . .]!
8 a-na EN-ME[Š-šú GUR]
9 DUG$_4$.DUG$_4$-ma [l]a [i-laq-qi] (U)
10f these lines (erased by scribe) contained the text of r8-9 by way of dittography
13 IGI ^{1}ZÁLAG!-a-a
14 ÌR ša L[Ú*!-. . .]
16 [IGI ^{1}]$^{.⸢d!⸣}$PA!-ZU! DUMU $^{1.d!}$PA!-[. .]
17 [IGI ^{1}]⸢ÌR!⸣-^{d}15 DUMU ^{1}⸢TA*! / ta⸣-///[. .]
18 [IGI ^{1}]⸢GÌR+2!⸣-/// DUMU ^{1}qi!-[. . .]
19 [IGI ^{1}. .]-⸢la!⸣-⸢a⸣-[a]
Edge 20 DUMU! ^{1}SUḪUŠ-[. . . .] (U)
21 ITU-ŠE UD-26-K[AM] (U)
22 lim-mu ^{1}I[T]U-AB-⸢a⸣-[a]
L.E. 23 DIB dan-ni-t[e]! (not -ti)
24 [. G]ÍN! KUG.UD ša UMBIN-šú (U)

ADD 258 (AR 65) Obv 2 [. . . .]/// šá URU-tar-bu-si-e (sic)
3 followed by a dividing line, unused space for stamp seal impressions or nail marks, and another dividing line
5 [^{1}(.).]/// 2 DUMU-MEŠ-šu
12 [UN-MEŠ] šu-a-⸢tú⸣ za-a[r!-p]u
13 [la-qi-u tu-a]-ru! de!-⸢e!⸣-[nu]
14 [DUG$_4$.DUG$_4$ la-áš-šú] ⸢man!⸣-nu [ša . .]
break
Rev 4' URU-tar-bu-si-e sic
6' ša!(not šá) É-GIBIL (U)

ADD 259 (AR 86) Obv 1 $^{1.d}$+EN-DUG$_4$.G[A]! (U)
3 $^{1.d!}$EN-AD-⸢PAB⸣ (U)
4 followed by a dividing line, unused space for stamp seal impressions, and another dividing line
7 [PAB . Z]I!-MEŠ
19 ina bur-ki šá ///
Rev 1 IGI ^{1}NU-TÉŠ-ba!-ana! L[Ú-. . .]
9 [ITU]-DU$_6$! (not DUL)

ADD 261 (AR 87) Obv 1' ^{MÍ}su-u-[. . .]⌜x x⌝[. . . . .] (U*)
2' 2 DUMU-MEŠ-šú DUMU.MÍ-su ⌜x⌝[. . . . .]
3' (end) ^{1}mad!-a-a [10-12 signs]!
4' (end) ^{1}si-t[i!- 10 signs]
5' PAB 20 LÚ-Z[I-MEŠ ÌR-MEŠ-ni]!
6' ša ^{URU}arba-ìl-a-a tu!-[piš-ma ^{MÍ}. . . . .]!
7' [^{MÍ}]⌜šá⌝-GIM!-tú ša [MURUB$_4$]-⌜URU!⌝[10 signs]!
8' ina ŠÀ ⌜8! MA.NA⌝[KUG.UD . . . .]
4 obliterated, virtually illegible lines
13'![. . . .] ⌜de⌝-e-[nu] ⌜DUG$_4$!⌝-[DUG$_4$ . . . .]
14' [. . . . . AN]ŠE!-KUR.RA-[MEŠ . . . .]
three illegible lines
Edge 18' [. . .] 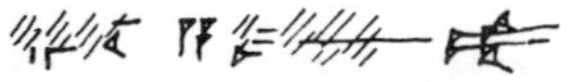 [ ]
Rev 3 LÚ*-mu-[ša]r-k[is]
5 LÚ*-ḫ[a-za]-nu
7 IGI $^{1.\text{d}}$PA-MAN-a-[ni LÚ*]-⌜šá!-UGU!⌝-URU ša URU-ni-nu-[a]
8 IGI ^{1}⌜na-ni⌝-i LÚ*-⌜A!.BA!⌝ ša DUMU-⌜LUGAL⌝
9 IGI ^{1}na-din!-la LÚ*-⌜DAM.QAR⌝ ANŠE-KUR.R[A-MEŠ]!
11 IGI $^{1.}$⌜$^{\text{d!}}$⌝[PA!-SIG$_5$]-iq ⌜LÚ*⌝-2-u
12 IGI ^{1}[. . . . .]-⌜da-ku?⌝ ša URU-ni-nu-a
13 IGI ^{1}[.]!-a-ni-⌜a!⌝ [LÚ*-šá-UG]U!-É-DINGIR-MEŠ
15 [IGI ^{1}. .]-PAB-PAB LÚ*!-3-[.]! ša
16 [IGI ^{1}. . .]-$^{\text{d!}}$[.]! LÚ*!-[. .] ša LÚ*-tur-ta-ni
17 [IGI ^{1}. . . .]⌜x x x⌝[.] DUMU URU-ni-nu-a

ADD 262 (AR 553) Obv 1'  ú-[p]iš-ma ^{1}[. . . .]
3' (at end) za-[ar-pu] (U)
5' (at end) lu-[u] 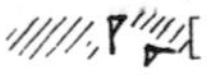[. . .]
7' (at end) TA* ^{1}30-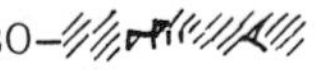
Rev 1-5 illegible
8 LÚ*- 
9 IGI ^{1}[. . .] LÚ*-[. . .]
10 IGI ^{1}[.]-la-mur LÚ*-[A.BA]
12 [ša] É! MÍ-É.GAL

ADD 263 (AR 175) Obv 2' 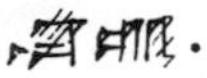. . . .(.) ^{MÍ}šá]-⌜kin!-tú! ša!⌝ MUR[UB$_4$!-URU]
3' ina ŠÀ 10 MA.[NA KUG.UD i]l-qi (U)
9' DUMU-MEŠ-šú DUMU-DUMU-MEŠ-šú sic
Rev 9 IGI ^{1}IM-⌜aš+šur!⌝
11 [IGI] ^{1}⌜EN!⌝-[. . .]

ADD 264 (AR 527)	Obv	1'	[de]-⌜e!⌝-nu! DUG$_4$.⌜DUG$_4$⌝ [la-áš-šú]
		2'	ina ma-te-e-me! (U)
		4'	la-a ad!(not a)-din (U)
	Rev	1	[IGI] $^{1.d}$UTU-MU!-SUM-na (U)
		3	sic
		4	IGI $^{1.d}$EN-(blank)[.]
		6	IGI ^{1}AN.GAL-me-[si] sic
			blank space of about 8 lines; the following two lines not written on edge!
		8	[. . . . .(.)]
ADD 265 (AR 75)	Obv		Beginning destroyed
			seal space with 1[+n] stamp seal impresssions
			——————————————!
		1'	[^{1}.]-nu!-lam!-ši! ^{1}EN-nu-r[i . .]⌜ÌR!⌝-[M]EŠ! [. .]
		2'	[$^{1.d}$]UTU-SU ^{MÍ}⌜bu-su-ku!⌝ MÍ-šú
		3'	^{1}i- 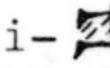 -na-a-a
		8'	šu-a-tu!( , not tú)
	Rev	7'	[i-ba]l!-a-kàt!()-ú-ni
		10'	[IGI ^{1}. .  -mal-ku-u-te! (U)
		11'	IGI ^{1}ḫi-⌜li⌝-ṣi!
ADD 269 (AR 63)	Obv	3	4 DUMU-M[EŠ!-š]ú!
		5	ú-pi[š-m]a!
	Rev	3'	[IGI ^{1}. . .]-⌜ib!⌝ LÚ-na-sik-ku
		4'	[IGI ^{1}m]ar!-da!-a-na
		9'	sic
ADD 272 (AR 526)	Obv	3	EN UN-MEŠ S[UM-ni]
			——————————!
			unused space for seals and nailmarks
		4	[
		5	[
			break(!)
	Rev	1'	[. . . . .] x x [. . . .]
		2'	[IGI ^{1}] 
		4'	IGI ^{1}DINGIR-lip!-ḫur (U)
ADD 274 (AR 69)	Obv	2	URU-KASKAL-a!-a! EN UN-MEŠ SUM-ni
			——————————————————!
			cylinder seal impression + stamp seal impression on edge
			——————————————————!
		3	[. . . . .]⌜x x⌝[^{d}]-⌜na-na-a!⌝ MÍ-šú

ADD 274 (AR 69) Obv 4 [. . . . .] 6 ZI-MEŠ
Rev 1' [. . . .] [. . .]
2' [IGI ^{1}. .]-a! LÚ*-A.[BA]
3' ITU-DUL(sic) UD-25!-KÁM
4' lim-mu ^{1}aš+šur!-KALAG-in-a-ni

ADD 277 (AR 62) Obv 1 NA$_4$-KIŠIB $^{1.⸢d⸣}$⸢AG!⸣-SU- . . .]
2 ⸢ÌR!⸣ LÚ!-⸢EN!⸣-[NAM] EN UN-MEŠ SU[M!-ni]
2[+2?] stamp seal impressions
3 (end) PAB ⸢2⸣ [0]
4 (end) PAB ⸢2⸣ [0]
5 (end) DUMU-MEŠ-šú [. . .]
6 [. . . . .] DUMU-šá PAB! [. . .]
7 [. . . . .] ⸢URU⸣[. . . .]
about half of obverse lost
Rev 1' [(.). . . .] ni [. . . .(.)]!
2' [. . . . .-M]EŠ!-šú ú-[ta-ra]!
3' [IGI ^{1}]⸢U+GUR!⸣-DÙ LÚ-3!-[šú]
10' [IGI] $^{1.d}$PA-⸢MU!⸣-[.] LÚ-A.BA ṣ[a-bit
Edge 11' [ITU-GU]D (U)
13' [LÚ!-GAR].KUR ša sa-ma!-[al-la]
L.E. 14' [. . . . .] [. .]

ADD 279 (AR 533) Obv 1 NA$_4$-KIŠIB ^{1}EN-KASKAL-
2 EN UN-MEŠ SUM-⸢ni⸣
two stamp seal impressions
3 [^{1}.]⸢x x -šu!⸣ ÌR-šú (U)
4 totally obliterated
5 [ú-piš-ma ^{1}. . . .]-⸢ni⸣ (U)
6 [TA* IGI ^{1}E]N-⸢KASKAL⸣-[.]-ṣur-a-ni
7 [. . .] 30! [. . .]
8 [. . . . .] TI
Rev 1' [ina]! de-ni-šú DUG$_4$.DUG$_4$-ma NU ⸢TI⸣ (U)
2' [IGI] ^{1}kan-dil-a-nu
3'-4' sic
5' (end) LÚ*!(not LÚ)-NAR
10' LÚ*!-GAR.KUR URU-sam-al-li (U)

ADD 284 (AR 462) Obv 1' [. . . . . .] -⌜da-a!⌝-a ⌜AMA⌝-šú
9' [a-na]! ⌜kal⌝ MU.AN.NA-MEŠ
10' i-zaq-qup-an-ni O! GIL-u-ni (U)
11' [ša! TA*] ^{1}DI-ma-nu-im-me
12' [lu-u DUMU]-DUMU-MEŠ-šú lu-u ⌜PAB⌝-MEŠ-[šú] (U)
Rev 1' [IGI ^{1}. .]-šal-lim LÚ-
6' [IGI ^{1}D]I!-KUR
7' [IGI $^{1.d}$P]A-TI-su-DUG$_4$!.GA (U)
11' [I]GI ^{1}ta-ga-li-i IGI $^{1.d}$PA-KÀD!-an-ni (U)
12' [IT]U-AB UD-28!-KÁM (sic; U -26-)

ADD 288 (AR 77) Obv Beginning destroyed; then seal space with no visible impressions and not followed by a dividing line
2' ^{1}ia-⌜nu⌝( )-qu DUMU-šú ⌜MÍ⌝-[. . . . . .]!
3' ^{1}da-⌜lu!⌝-ú!-a! DUMU-šú MÍ-š[ú . .]!
4' sic
5' ^{MÍ}d[i]-im-ba!-⌜a?⌝ [. . . .]
6' ^{1}da-⌜di!-i!⌝ [. . . .]
8' PAB [. . . . . .]
Rev 1' [ina de-ni]!-⌜šú! DUG$_4$⌝.DUG$_4$-[ma . . .] (U*)
3' sic
5' IGI $^{1.d!}$30-ṣa-⌜la!-a!⌝ [. .]
6' IGI ^{1}DÙG-IM-^{d}1[5 . .]!
7' IGI $^{1.d}$PA-PAB-AŠ [. . .]!
8' IGI ^{1}DÙG.GA-É!-^{d}15 [. .] (U)
11' IGI ^{1}mi-i-su [. . . .]
12' [IGI] ^{1}ḫal-li-ṣi! [. . . . .] (U)
Edge 13' (end) šúm-mu [. . .]!
14' [. . . . .] la i-din

ADD 293 (AR 555) Obv Beginning destroyed, then seal space with traces of 1[+n] stamp seal impression
———————————————————!
1' ^{1}[. . .]-a-a [. . .(.)]!
2' ^{MÍ}ḪAL!-⌜a!⌝-ni-^{d}[. . . .]!
4' ú-piš-ma ^{1} [. . . .]
6' sic
7' (end) KUG.UD [. .]!
8' i-zi-rip i-TI-qi ma-[. .]!
9'
10'
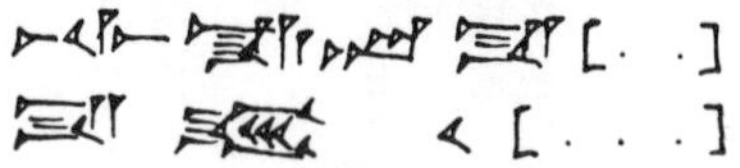

ADD 293 (AR 555) Edge uninscribed
Rev 1 [. . .]! šu!-a-t[ú]! ⌜za!⌝-[ar-pu la-qi-u]!
2 [. . . .] la!-[áš-šú . . . .]
balance destroyed

ADD 294 (AR 49) Obv 1! [NA$_4$-KIŠIB ^{1}. . . . .]
2! EN [MÍ-MEŠ ta-da-ni]
———————————!
2[+1] stamp seal impressions
———————————!
3! ^{MÍ}AŠ!-qi-di!-ra MÍ-[. . . . .]
7! [LÚ]-⌜qur!-bu!⌝- ti ša! [. . .] (U)
8! [ina ŠÀ . MA].NA! KUG!.[UD . .] (U)
Rev 1' [IGI ^{1}.
2' [IGI ^{1}]a-a-PAB-MEŠ LÚ*-EN[GAR! . . .]
3'-5' end: LÚ*-ENGA[R . . .]
8' IGI ^{1}šá!-a-da URU-[. . .] (U)
9' ^{1}a-me-qi sic
Edge 12' [IGI] $^{1.d}$ [. . . . .]

ADD 295 (AR 498) Obv 1! [NA$_4$-KIŠIB ^{1}. . . . .]
2! [ ]
———————————!
stamp seal impression
———————————!
3! ^{MÍ}la-ṣa!-ḫi!-⌜i!⌝-[ti . . .]
4! sic
6! ina ŠÀ-bi 5! [. . . . .]
Rev 2-3 spaced out
6 ^{1}10-DÙG!.GA! [. . .]
7 ^{1}qur-d[i!-. . .]
8 ^{1}pa-
9 IGI ^{1}⌜i!⌝-[. . . .]
remainder lost
Edge 1 ITU-BARAG UD-15 sic

ADD 296 (AR 79) Obv 1! destroyed
2! [E]N UN-M[EŠ
———————————!
two stamp seal impressions
———————————!
4 ^{1}-ḫu!-la!-a-a ^{1}ma-ri-li-ḫi!
6 (end) ša ^{1}⌜mar?⌝-]
Rev 1' [IGI ^{1}. .] -la-a-[a . . .] (both -a]l!- and -t]al- seem possible

ADD 296 (AR 79) Rev 2' IGI ^{1}SU-ba!-a-a! [. .]

3' IGI ^{1}a-a-am-me [. . .]!

4' IGI ^{1}U.U!-DÙ [. . .]!

5' IGI ^{1}tu!-⌜im!⌝-mu [. . .]

6' IGI $^{1.}$⌜d!⌝ [.]-šė-zib L[Ú*!-. .]

7' IGI ^{1}10-rém-a-ni L[Ú*!-. .]

blank space of ca. 7 lines

8' [ITU]-[illegible] [UD-.] ⌜lim!⌝-[mu . . . .]!

ADD 298 (AR 534) Obv 1 [NA$_4$]-KIŠIB $^{1.d}$ra-man-[illegible]

2 [E]N UN-MEŠ SUM-a-ni

______________________________!

3 stamp seal impressions

______________________________!

balance of obverse destroyed

Rev 2' [IGI ^{1}P]AB!-BÀD (U)

3' [IGI ^{1}.][illegible]-zi-iz! (U)

two lines blank; date

ADD 300 (AR 545) Obv 2 followed by a dividing line, 1[+n] stamp seal impressions, and another dividing line

Rev 1' [. .][illegible] kas!-p[u! . . . .]

2' [ina de-n]i!-⌜šú!⌝ DU[G$_4$.DUG$_4$-ma . . . .] (U)

____

5' [IGI] ^{1}se!-na!-[illegible] . . .]

7' [IGI] ^{1}ia-P[AB!-MEŠ] (U)

10' before date, one line blank

ADD 301 (AR 535) Obv 1 [NA$_4$-KIŠ]IB ^{1}[illegible] -du!-u-a LÚ*-GAL-U[RU]! (cf. ADD 306:1 f; ^{1}⌜i⌝-du-u-a possible though traces do look like ^{1}ni-)

3 [EN] UN-MEŠ ta-da-ni

==============================!

cylinder seal impression

____

4 [^{1}. . . .]-⌜a!⌝ LÚ*-ENGAR

5 [ ] ⌜LÚ*!⌝-ENGAR!

Rev 3 preceded by a blank space (about 1 line wide)

ADD 308 (AR 57) Obv 1 [NA$_4$-KIŠIB ^{1}.-i]a!-ka-a- [illegible] -a 0! (the sign between the two a's is pressed and therefore perhaps meant to be ignored)

3 [EN] MÍ ta-SUM-ni (U)

______________________________!

three stamp seal impressions

______________________________!

ADD 308 (AR 57) Obv 6 sic
7 ^{1}tar-ḫu-na-zi ÌR!-šu! (U)
10 za-O!-pat là!-TI (U)
Rev 1 TA*!(not TA) ^{1}ka-ku-la-nu
9 IGI ^{1}ba-la-si O! A $^{1.d}$PA!-na-kil :!-ma!
12 LÚ*-GIŠ.GIGIR MAN!
14 [IGI ^{1}ḫ]i-ri-⌜ṣa⌝-a-a (U)
Edge 16 [IGI $^{1.d}$U]TU-ma!-PAB (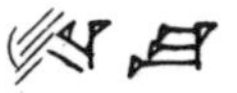)

ADD 309 (AR 56) Obv Beginning destroyed; then seal space (with no extant impressions)
———————————————!
1' ^{MÍ}a-bi-d/ṭa-l[i/l[a- ()
Rev 5' IGI ^{1}i-di-i KUR-kiš-q[a!-a-a] (cf. ADD 357 r10)
9' lim-mu ^{1} [. . .] (uncertain whether ^{1}N[U!- or ^{1}⌜ṣal!⌝-)
10' LÚ*-tur-ta-nu KUR-k[u!-mu-ḫi]

ADD 310 (AR 158) Obv 1 [N]A$_{4}$!-KIŠIB $^{1.d}$IM-P[AB!-AŠ]
2 [EN] UN-MEŠ SUM-n[i]!
———————————————!
two stamp seal impressions
———————————————!
3 [^{1}].⌜d⌝[U].GUR-K[A]L-an $^{MÍ!}$⌜15!⌝- [. MÍ-šú]
4 [^{M}]^{Í}mar-ti-i :! $^{MÍ!}$ma-ár-a-s[a]!
5 3 ru-u-[ṭ]u [la-an-šá]
6 PAB 3 ZI-[MEŠ ÌR-MEŠ š]a [$^{1.d}$IM-PAB-AŠ] (U)
7 ú-piš-⌜ma⌝ [$^{1!}$man-nu-ki-i]!-^{d}⌜al⌝-l[a!-a-a]
8 rak-[s]u
10 ša URU-ga-⌜ár!⌝-sa(sic!)-me-si! TI
11 ur-ki ⌜da!-ra!⌝-ri UN-MEŠ a-si-qi (sic)
12 kas()-pu ⌜ga⌝-[mur] ta-din
15 [l]a-⌜áš⌝-š[ú man-nu] ⌜ša⌝ ina ur-kiš
16 [ina ma-te-ma] ⌜lu-u⌝ $^{1.d}$IM-PAB-AŠ
17 [lu-u DUMU-MEŠ-šú lu-u DUMU]-DUMU-MEŠ-šú (U)
Edge 19 [. . .]! pa-nu-u' sic (spaced out)
Rev 1 [TA* $^{1!}$]man-nu-
5 a-šib (sic) URU-NINA :! GAR-an GIŠ-BAN G[Ú!+UN]
7 (end) GAL-⌜u!⌝
9 (end) DÙG.GA-MEŠ-⌜te!⌝
10 a-na be-la-tu-ṣe-e-ri (sic) : i-qa!-m[u]!
11 [kas-p]u ... u-GU[R] sic
12 [ina!] de-nu(sic)-šú

ADD 310 (AR 158) Rev 13 [be]-⸢e!⸣-nu (U)
14 [sa-a]r-tu a-na MU.AN.NA-ME[Š]! (U)

---

16 [IGI ^{1}ma]n!-nu-ki-URU-ni-nu-a PAB 4! IGI-ME[Š]
17 [. . .] 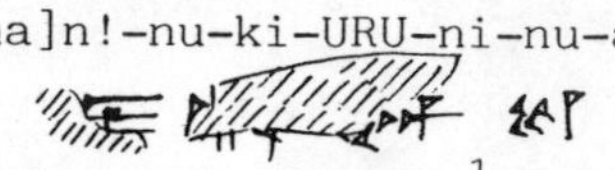
18 [IGI ^{1}ta-b]al!-a-a IGI ^{1}pu-ḫi-i [0]
20 [IGI ^{1}i]z!-bu IGI ^{1}ta-li!-[.]

ADD 311 (AR 53) Obv 2 LÚ-ÌR ša $^{1.d}$⸢UTU!-MAN!⸣-a!-ni
3 followed by a dividing line, 3 stamp seal impressions, and another dividing line
7 ^{1}ab-d[u]-⸢nu⸣ DUMU! $^{1!}$ku!-ku-ul!-[la]-a-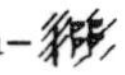
Rev 11, 13, 18 sic
L.E. I 1 IGI ^{1}ÌR-15 A ^{1}ḫ[a!-ri]-ru!-⸢ri!⸣ (U*)
2 IGI ^{1}sin-qi A ^{1}GIN-i! IGI! ⸢x x x⸣
3 IGI ^{1}di-lil-15 A ^{1}bu-a!-di-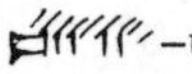-u
II 1 IGI ^{1}[. . .-a-a-u
2 ⸢ITU⸣-[.] UD-14-KAM
3 l[i-mu] $^{1.d}$ŠÚ-MAN-PAB (U)

ADD 312 (AR 467) Obv 2 EN MÍ [ta-da]-⸢a!⸣-ni

---!

two stamp seal impressions

---!

3 sic
9 O! ša GIL-u-ni
10 [lu-u ^{1}DINGIR-ia]-a-u (U)
balance of obverse lost (!)
Rev 1 d[e-n]u DUG_4.D[UG_4] ⸢ub⸣-ta-u-⸢ni⸣
3 ina EN-šú! (no MEŠ after EN !)
12 IGI ^{1}ÌR-^{d}GAŠAN! (U)
14 IGI ^{1}ḫal-li-[i LÚ*]-DAM!.QAR! (U)

ADD 316 (AR 74) Obv 1' (end) 4 ⸢ru!⸣-ṭ[u]! (U*)
2' [. . ^{1}]ú-si-a
3' [^{1}.]-⸢$^{d!}$⸣15 pir-su ^{MÍ}ba-a-as-si DUMU.MÍ [. . .]!
6' [^{1}mil]-ki-ZÁLAG
7' $^{1.d}$ŠÚ-man-re-man-ni sic (cf. 5'!)

ADD 320 (AR 529) Obv 1 [(.). . . ^{1}]ur!-du ^{1}a[m!-. . . .] (U*)
2 [(.). . . .]-a-a ^{1}na-a'-[di-. .]

---!

three fingernail impressions

---!

ADD 320 (AR 529) Obv 3 ^{1}URU! (wr.)-tuk-la!-a-tú-u-a
Edge 7 74 MA.NA (sic; U: 75) URUDU-MEŠ i[l-q]i
8 DI.KUD sic
Rev 3 SUḪUŠ written

ADD 321 (AR 659) Obv Beginning destroyed, then blank space for seals
———————————————!
1' ⌜ú!⌝-ma-a it-ta-a[[t]]-ru-uṣ sic
2' [is]-sa-ḫi-iš ^{MÍ}KUR-a-di-im-ri sic
3' [DU]MU.MÍ-su
4' [L]Ú a-na!
10' 10 MA.NA ⌜KUG⌝.U[D SU]M!-⌜an!⌝ AN.ŠÁR ^{d}UTU (U*)
11' [. . . . .] [.]
edge and possibly last and first lines of Obv. and Rev. (respectively) broken away
Rev 1' lim-m[u . . . .]
2' ^{1}AN.ŠÁR-DÙ-A MA[N . . . . .]
3' blank LÚ-GA[L-. . . .] sic (U:)
4' IGI ^{1}a-da-lal LÚ-DUMU-ŠU+? šá! [ ]
5' I[GI $^{1.d}$I]M-ba-ba-u (sic) LÚ-DUMU ŠU!2!
7' IGI ^{1}⌜aš+šur!⌝-DINGIR-a-a
8' [ ]
9' [ ]-ḫu!

ADD 322 (AR 200) Obv 1! completely destroyed
2! [EN] ⌜UN⌝-[M]EŠ [. . .]
———————————————!
cylinder seal impression
———————————————!
3! [^{1}..]-a!-DÙG!+G[A]! ÌR-šú
4! [^{1}...]-DINGIR!-a-a MÍ-šú
5! [. . .]-a!-tú DUMU.MI-su
8! [dan-nu ša ^{1}aš-šur]-DÙ!-A LUGAL O!
11! [ilqi UN-MEŠ . .] zar!-[pu . . .] (U)
Rev 1' [. . . .]-MEŠ! [. . . . .]
2' [ina de-ni-šú] i-da-bu-u[b!-ma la i-laq]-qí!
3' [de-en-šú LÚ]-da-a-a-ni l[a! i-š]e!-[m]e!
———————————————
4' [IGI ^{1}sa-']i!-ru LÚ-3.U$_{5}$
5' [IGI $^{1.d}$P]A!-ši-me-an LÚ-3.U$_{5}$
6' [IGI $^{1.d}$]EN!-ú!-<<< LÚ-ḫa-za-nu
7' [IGI] $^{1.⌜d!⌝}$U+GUR!-DINGIR-⌜a!-a!⌝ LÚ!-A.BA!
8' [IGI ^{1}ḫ]u-ba-šá-a-te LÚ-šá-U.U!
9' [IGI ^{1}]⌜a!⌝-kul-la-a-nu

ADD 324 (AR 36) Obv 4 LÚ*!(not LÚ)-3-šú ša a-rit

5 EN É SUM-an sic

---!

4 small (6x9 mm) elliptical circles, possibly to be taken as unusual nailmarks

---!

7 TÙR written 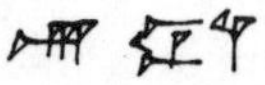

Rev 3 ^{1}EN-BAD! (sic! BAD for BÀD owing to lack of space)

4 kas!-pu! (U)

6 de-e-ni u DUG$_4$.DUG$_4$ sic

7 la-aš-šu! (not -šú) (U)

8 an-nu-ti! (not -te) (U)

12, 14 sic

16 LÚ*-GAL!-MÁ.DU.DU (U)

17 (end) IGI ^{1}zi- 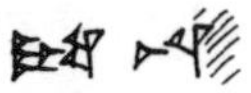

L.E. 2 LÚ*!(not LÚ)-GAR.KUR

3 $^{1.d}$PA-MU-AŠ!

ADD 327 (AR 358) Obv 1' É GIŠ-4-IG ⌜a⌝ [. .] sic (for 4 GIŠ-IG)

2' ina ŠÀ-bi  . .]

Rev 2 i-za-qup-pan!-a-ni (U)

10, 11 (at end) :! :! (not ⁝ ⁝)

13 IGI ^{1}su-nu-[. .] (room for two signs at most)

14! IGI! $^{1!}$[. . . . .]

balance of Reverse lost

ADD 328 (AR 357) Obv 1 (at end) ^{1}TA*-^{d}ŠÚ- 

6 (at end) $^{1.d}$UTU-⌜ú!-bal!-liṭ!⌝

8 ^{1}man-nu-ki-i!-PAB-MEŠ

15 ša TA*! (not TA) ^{1}S[U-DINGIR-MEŠ-ni . . . .]

two lines + edge lost

Rev 3 ^{1}du-gul-IGI-DING[IR] L[Ú*!-. .]

4 ša gi-né-šú š[a . .] sic

6 LÚ*-GAL-50 ša 

7 sic

9 LÚ*-NAGAR-GIŠ-UMBI[N]-⌜MEŠ!⌝

12 after this line, blank space of about 4 lines

14 lim!-mu (not li-mu)

ADD 329 (AR 359) Obv 1 ^{1}bi-ir!-a-tar

5 mu-ṣu-u is-sa-ḫi!-si (sic)

8 ^{1}ḫa-na!-ḫu-ru

ADD 329 (AR 359) Obv 10 [ina ŠÀ-bi] GÍN KUG.UD il-qi (30-60 possible)
Rev 1 i-za-qu-p[a!-ni]
2 [. . . . .] šú! SUM-an
8 IGI ^{1}za- -nu
10 IGI ^{1} -ma-nu (probably ^{1}DIL!-ma-nu, with accidental winkelhaken)
14 sic

ADD 330 (AR 195) Obv 2 followed by a dividing line, cylinder seal impression, and another dividing line
4 (end) URU- -⌜da⌝-da
5 tak!-pi-[. . . .]
15-16 completely obliterated
17 [TA*! ^{1}]man-nu-k[i-URU-arba-ìl]
18 ⌜ù!⌝ DUMU-MEŠ-šú (U)
19 2! MA.NA KUG.UD
Rev 1 a-ši-pat! URU-arba-ìl S[UM!-an] (U*)
4 de-e-šú! (U) sic
10 LÚ*-ra-ka-su sic
15 this line in smaller script than the rest

ADD 332 (AR 360) 1 followed by dividing line, 3[+n] horizontal finger-nail impressions, and another dividing line
2 [ṣ]u-pur ^{1}GÌR+2-^{d}⌜15!⌝ [EN É ta-da-ni] (U)
4 (end) maš- [. . .]
Rev 1' [4 ANŠE-ḫar-b]a!-kan!-⌜ni!⌝ [. . . . . .]
2' [. MA.NA KUG].UD! a-na bu[r-ki . . . . .] (U)
9' [IGI] ^{1}SUḪUŠ-^{d}U+G[UR]!
10' [IGI] ^{1}sa-ka-a[' . . .]!
12' [DUMU?] (space) URU-NINA-[KI]
3 lines blank
13' IGI ^{1}tab-ni-^{d}[. . LÚ!-A.BA!]
14' [ṣa]!-bit ṭup-pi I[TU!-. . . .]
15' [li]m!-mu ^{1}DI-[. . . . .]

ADD 333 (AR 339) Obv 2 sic
————————————————!
3 stamp seal impressions
————————————————!
3 [É ri-p]i-tú a-na gi-mir-tú-[šá ..] sic
4 [. . . . šá
5 [. . . .] ⌜ina! URU!⌝- [. . . . . .]

ADD 333 (AR 339) Rev 1' [IGI ^{1}. . .]-⸢^{d}!IM!⸣ URU!-[. . . .]
4' [IGI ^{1}IT]U!-AB-a-a IGI ^{1}[. . . .]
5' [IGI ^{1}š]á!-kil-ia ša URU-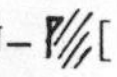[. . . .]
7' ITU-ŠE UD-12-KÁM l[im!-mu]
Edge 9' DI-mu ina bir-t[u!-šú-nu
12' [IGI ^{1}]dan-ni-⸢i!⸣ [. .]
L.E. 1 IGI ^{1}tar-d[i!-. . . . . . .]

ADD 335 (AR 337) Obv 1 completely destroyed
2! EN É SUM-ni
!
one(!) large (12 x 25 mm) stamp seal impression
!
3! 3 É ŠU+⸢2-MEŠ!⸣ TÙR [0]
7! gab-di $^{1.d}$+PA-u+a (written 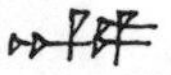 )
9! ^{1}di-li[l!-DN]
Rev 1 TA* IGI ^{1}DI.KUD-kur-ba-⸢il!⸣ ()
5 sic
6 ⸢tú⸣-a-ru de-⸢e!⸣-nu
10 IGI ^{1}ÌR-⸢^{d}!⸣[. .(.)]-tin!(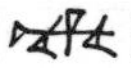)-ni

ADD 337 (AR 178) Obv 2 URU-ma-ga-ni-⸢ib!⸣()
3 sic
!
cylinder seal impression
!

5 [. . .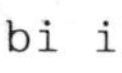 1 A-MEŠ! bi il?(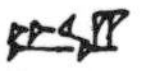) kan na ki-qi!-il-te
8 [kaq-qi-ri p]u!-ṣe-e 30 GÍD!.D[A]!
Rev 2' [ina bur-ki ^{d}NI]N!.LÍL GAR-an
3' [2 ANŠE-KUR.RA]! BABBAR-MEŠ (U)
4' [0] KEŠDA!
7' [IGI ^{1}. . .] A-SIG šá ⸢GAŠAN!⸣-É 0! šá DUMU-MAN (U*)

ADD 338 (AR 355) Obv 1' 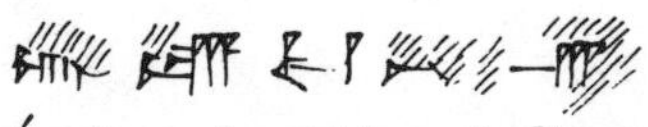
2' É-ub-sa!-a-ti qa!-[ba-sa-a-ti] (U*)
3' a-di ÍL!-t[i . . . .] ()
8' ⸢LÚ*!⸣-EN!.N[AM! . . .]
last two lines of Obverse, Edge, and first two lines of Reverse lost
2' TA*! DU[MU]!-MEŠ!-šú! [. . . .]
3' ub-[ta]-⸢u⸣-ni 10 [. . . . .] (U)
4' ⸢a!⸣-n[a]! ⸢^{d}⸣IM a-šib URU-[. . . .]
5' [ka]s!-⸢pu!⸣ a-na 10-MEŠ-te (U)

ADD 338 (AR 355) Rev 6' [ina de-ni-š]ú! DUG$_4$.DUG$_4$-[ma . . .]
——————————————————!
balance of Rev. lost
L.E.2 [E]N.NAM ša ⌜É⌝ [.]////[. .]

ADD 343 (AR 363) Obv 2a ——————————!
3 stamp seal impressions
——————————!
3 É ep-šú a-di GIŠ-ÙR-MEŠ-š[ú]!
5-6 sic
9 SUḪUR e-nu É šá! bu [. . .] (U)
10 it-ta- 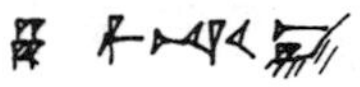

ADD 345 (AR 365) Rev 2' IGI ^{1}ZU-te!(not -ti)-DINGIR (U)
3' IGI ^{1}ag-da-áš-DINGIR LÚ-ŠIMxA!
Edge 8' LÚ-DIB-KUŠ-O!-MEŠ : (U)
9' 22 GÍD.DA 18! DAGAL

ADD 348 (AR 367) Obv 1' [. . . .] qa!-an-ni! [. . .]
3' [. . is]-sa-ḫi-iš e-ru!-š[u! . . . .]
8' [ú piš ma ^{1}li]a lıu la [nu . .]

ADD 350 (AR 165) Obv 2a ——————————————!
3[+n] vertical fingernail impressions
——————————————!
3 kaq-qi-ri pu-[ṣe-e (.).]//// -i!
15 lu-u ŠEŠ!(not PAB)-šú
16 ⌜TA!⌝ (not TA*)
Edge 17 de-nu!(not -ni) DUG$_4$.DUG$_4$ ub-ta-'u-O!-[ni]
Rev 1 (end) MA.NA K[UG.GI]
4 ANŠE-ḫar-b[a!-kan-ni]
5 ú-še-[rab 1 GU+UN]
6 AN.NA a-na LÚ*-šak-nu (sic) [URU-šú SUM-an]
7 kas-pu a-na 1-me-⌜ni! a⌝-[na EN-šú]
8 D[UG$_4$.DUG$_4$-ma . . .]
——————————
9 IGI ^{1}I-DINGIR ⌜LÚ*!⌝-////[. . .]
11 PAB 4 IGI-MEŠ URU-[. . .]-a-a
——————————————!
12 IGI $^{1.d}$⌜U.GUR-DÙ⌝ O! ^{1}⌜$^{.d}$IM-MU-PAB⌝
13 IGI ^{1}⌜pu-u⌝-[lu IGI ^{1}]⌜$^{.d!}$⌝šá-maš-////-da-a
15 IGI ^{1}⌜SANGA!⌝-^{d}15 LÚ*-A.⌜BA⌝

ADD 351 (AR 336) Obv 1 NA$_4$-KIŠIB ^{1}ša-DINGIR-ta!-za-⌜az!⌝
4a ————————————————!
two stamp seal impresssions
————————————————!
6 ⌜5!⌝ ina!+1 KÙŠ DAGAL
Rev 2 il-qí! (not -qi)
4 [šu-a]-tú! pat!-[.(.)] 
5 [. . . . .] lim-me ^{1}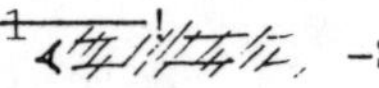 -SU

ADD 352 (AR 349) Obv 2 A ^{1}ḫur-ru-ṣ[u . . .]!
Rev 1' ⌜GAR!-an!⌝ kas-pu a-na 10+ME!-t[e! a-na EN-šú]
4' IGI ^{1}ra-ḫi-mu-U.U! LÚ*-mu-kil-KUŠ-PA-ME[Š .]-kal!
5' IGI ^{1}M[AN-IGI.L]AL-a-ni LÚ*-3-si :! :! (not ⁝ ⁝)
6' IGI [^{1}. . .]-⌜ram!⌝-ma
8' ^{1}MAN-NUMUN!() ša-GÌR+2 A-MAN!
L.E. 2! [IGI ^{1}b]a!-da!-a
4! [IGI $^{1.d}$P]A!-DI-PAB-MEŠ

ADD 353 (AR 335) Obv 1 ⌜ku⌝-[u]m NA$_4$-KIŠIB-šú ⌜ṣu⌝-p[ur-šú iš-kun]
————————————————!
4 horizontal fingernail impressions
————————————————!
2 ṣu-pur $^{1.d}$AG-še-zib-a-ni [. .]!
6 [SUḪUR A.Š]À $^{1.d}$⌜AG!⌝-[. . .]
Rev 1'! ⌜IGI!⌝[. . . . . .]
3 lines blank
2'! IGI $^{1.d}$30-AD-PAB L[Ú]-A.[BA]
4'! lim-mu ^{1}DINGIR-MAN!-[a-ni]

ADD 354 (AR 348) Obv 1' [. . . .] nu! sa ⌜a!⌝[. . . . .] (U*)
3' [SUHUR] $^{1!}$qi-li-i SUḪUR ⌜É!⌝ [^{1}. . .]
5' [ša]! ⌜Ú!⌝-SAR
6' [SUḪUR] $^{⌜1!⌝}$ma-ḫi-te-e PAB-ma O!
Rev 1 ⌜ú-piš⌝ O ^{1}UD-20-KÁM-a-a sic
9 [GI]L!-u-ni
L.E.3 ni!-[

ADD 357 (AR 345) Obv 1' [ú-piš]-ma ^{1}bar!-[di]-⌜i⌝ (U*)
3' 5 ½ M[A.N]A K[UG].UD ina 1! MA.NA! (not -né-e) ša MAN
Rev 3 -⌜šú⌝ at end of line uncertain, perhaps damage only
10 URU-kiš-qa-a-a sic
11 [IGI . . .]-a-a : : O!
12 [IGI . . .]x-NUMUN IGI ^{1}[. . . . . .] MÍ-É.GAL !

ADD 358 (AR 344)　　Obv 1　　[NA₄]-KIŠIB ¹EN-ŠU.SI(sic)-šá- ⟨cuneiform⟩

　　　　　　　　　　　　　2　　[:]! ¹PAB-la-mur (no room for NA₄-KIŠIB!)

　　　　　　　　　　　　4a　————————————————!
　　　　　　　　　　　　　　　2[+1] stamp seal impressions (!)

　　　　　　　　　　Rev 1'　　[. . . .] ⟨cuneiform⟩

　　　　　　　　　　　　4'　　[IGI ¹ . . . . .] A!-MAN

　　　　　　　　　　　　9'　　[IGI ¹·ᵈP]A-TI-E

　　　　　　　　　Edge 10'　　[IGI ¹b]al-ṭa-a

　　　　　　　　　　　11'　　[O! LÚ*]-GAL-50

　　　　　　　　　　　12'　　[IGI ¹]ÌR-na-na-a

　　　　　　　　　　　13'　　[O]!　　　A.BA

ADD 359 (AR 372)　　Obv 2　　LÚ*-A.⌜BA!⌝ (⟨cuneiform⟩)

　　　　　　　　　　　　3　　ša GIŠ-til-lit-[ti]! SUM-ni
　　　　　　　　　　　　　————————————————!
　　　　　　　　　　　　　unused space for stamp seal impressions
　　　　　　　　　　　　　————————————————!

　　　　　　　　　　　　4　　GIŠ-SAR ša GIŠ-til-lit-ti! (U)

　　　　　　　　　　　　8　　SUḪUR ⟨cuneiform⟩ bur-ti!

　　　　　　　　　　　　9　　[⟨cuneiform⟩]

　　　　　　　　　　　14　　⌜SU]M-ni

　　　　　　　　　Edge 16　　[de-nu]! DUG₄.DUG₄ (no space for -e-)

　　　　　　　　　　Rev 14　　sic (wr. ⟨cuneiform⟩

　　　　　　　　　　　15　　sic

　　　　　　　　　　　16　　¹da-ia!-a O! (U*)

ADD 363 (AR 371)　　Obv 1　　NA₄-KIŠIB ¹qu-u-a-a! DUMU [¹]- ⟨cuneiform⟩. . .]

　　　　　　　　　　　　2　　URU-tar-qa-na-a-a EN GIŠ-[SAR SUM-ni]
　　　　　　　　　　　　　————————————————!
　　　　　　　　　　　　　cylinder seal impression
　　　　　　　　　　　　　————————————————!

　　　　　　　　　　　　3　　[GI]Š-SAR ša til-lit-te! [. .] (U*)

　　　　　　　　　　　　4　　[ina! ŠÀ! UR]U-tu-ur-s[a-na . .]

　　　　　　　　　　Rev 1'　　IG[I . . . . IGI] ¹tar-di-tú- ⟨cuneiform⟩

　　　　　　　　　L.E. 1　　A-MEŠ qa-n[i! . . . .]

ADD 365 (AR 370)　　Obv 3a　————————————————!
　　　　　　　　　　　　　5 horizontal fingernail impressions
　　　　　　　　　　　　　————————————————!

　　　　　　　　　　　　4　　[GI]Š-SAR ša Ú-SAR URU-kal-gu-rig? (⟨cuneiform⟩)

　　　　　　　　　　　　6　　[¹. . ⟨cuneiform⟩ -ši

　　　　　　　　　　　　7　　[. .(.) il-qi kas-pu gam]-mur O!

　　　　　　　　　　Rev 1'　　[kas-pu ana] 10-MEŠ-te ⌜a!-na!⌝ [EN-šú GUR]

　　　　　　　　　　　4'　　IGI ¹ki!-ni-iḫ-ma-a

ADD 366 (AR 52)	Obv 2	LÚ-NU.GIŠ.SAR ÌR L[Ú!-. . .]
	3	EN GIŠ-SAR-MEŠ [. . .]
		————————————————!
		2![+1] stamp seal impressions
	Rev 5'	IGI $^{1.d}$PA-⌜KUR!⌝-u-a
ADD 367 (AR 390)	Obv 1	NA$_4$-KIŠIB $^{1.d}$U.GUR-ú-[b]al-liṭ-su
	2	NA$_4$-KIŠIB $^{1.d}$U.GUR-up!-[n]i!-ia (U)
	5	[EN] GIŠ-SAR šá ⌜Ú!⌝-[SAR . . . . SUM-n]i!
		unused space for seal impressions
	Rev 1'	[IGI ^{1}]$^{.⌜d⌝}$PA-še-zib LÚ-[. . . . .]
		remainder (about 6 lines) blank (!)
ADD 370 (AR 114)	Obv 3	[PA]B 2 LÚ-MEŠ-e
		————————————————!
		cylinder seal impression
	Rev 1'	[. . . . . .] LÚ*-ÌR ša ⌜LÚ*!-EN!⌝-[NAM]
	3'	after date, one line blank
	4'	[šá] GIŠ-SAR
	5'	[l]a i-na-su-ḫu il-ku!
	6'	TA*!(not TA) URU!-šú! la! il-lak (U*)
ADD 371 (AR 387)	Obv 1	⌜ṣu-pur⌝ ^{1}PAB-DINGIR-⌜a!-a!⌝ [. . . .]! (U)
	2	EN GIŠ-SAR [. . . SUM-n]i!
		————————————————!
		7 fingernail impressions
		————————————————!
	3	[. . .] lim! GIŠ!-til!-lit!-te ina! URU!-me!-du!- 
	4	[. . . . .] ^{1}pi-⌜qa⌝-qi (sic)
	Rev 1'	[. . . . . . .] ⌜si!⌝ ad! [. .]
	2'	[. . . . . .]⌜x⌝ ša! URU!-ir/sa!-ri!
	3'	[IGI] ^{1}SAG!.DU!-a!-nu LÚ*-SAG
	4'	IGI ^{1}⌜qur⌝-di-10 URU!-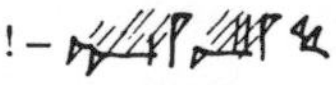-a-a
	5'	[IG]I! $^{1!}$ana-ku (rest of line blank)
	Edge 6'	[ITU]-DUL UD-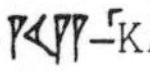-⌜KAM⌝[. . . . .]
ADD 372 (AR 389)	Obv 2'	[la-qi-u! tu-a-ru d]e-nu! (not -ni) DUG$_4$.DUG$_4$ la-áš-šú
	10'	[la ta-ad-din A.ŠÀ-ME]Š! GIŠ-SA[R-ME]Š!
	11'	[UN-MEŠ la za-ar-pu] la [la-qi-u]!
		remainder destroyed
	Rev 1'	[. . . . . .]⌜A!.TA!⌝.[ÀM]
	2'	[a-na EN-šú GUR i]na! la de-ni-[šú]
	3'	[DUG$_4$.DUG$_4$-ma la T]I-qí
		————————————

ADD 373 (AR 400) Obv 3 TA* written
4a ——————————————————!
unused(!) space for stamp seal impressions
——————————————————!
5 sic
Rev 1 laq-qí! (not -qi) (U)
2 ta-ti-din sic
3 laq-qí! (U)
Edge 15 ú-ta!-r[a] (U)

ADD 376 (AR 430) Obv Beginning destroyed; then unused(!) space for seal impressions
——————————————————!
2' SUḪUR ḫa-[. . .]
3' SUḪUR ⌈na⌉-ḫal-li [. . . . .]
4' SUḪUR KASKAL ša [a-na] URU--ú!-te!
5' DU-u-ni
6' SUḪUR ⌈É⌉ ^{1}za!-⌈ba!⌉-a!-a
7' SUḪUR É ^{1}⌈qi!⌉-di-ni
8' an-nu-u-te SUḪUR-MEŠ! ša! É!
11' ša KUR-e sic
Edge uninscribed (no il-qi)
Rev 2 (end) za-⌈ri!⌉-i[p]!
3 la-qi man-nu ša 0! ur-kiš (U)
6 2 ⌈MA!.NA!⌉ KUG.GI (U)
7 ina bu-ur-ki ^{d}[iš-t]ar! a-ši-pat (U)
8 URU-arba-ìl-KI i!-š[ak!-kan]! kas-pu ina 10-MEŠ 0!
9 ina ⌈EN⌉-MEŠ-šú [GUR.RA]! ina de-ni-šú
10 i-da-bu-[bu] la i-laq-⌈qi⌉
(no dividing line!)
11 [de-en-šú DI.KUD la i-š]á!-m[u]!-u
L.E. 1 10-tú nu-sa-ḫi! ù [. . . . .] (U*)

ADD 377 (AR 399) Obv 1' ⌈EN! É!⌉[. . . . S]UM-ni
——————————————————
unused space for stamp seal impressions
——————————————————
3' 0! a-⌈na⌉ URU-ŠE- ^{1}il-di-ši
4' [. . . k]a!-MEŠ SUḪUR A.ŠÀ ša ^{1}lu!-[. . .]
5' [. . . . .]⌈^{1}⌉SUM!-na-a
6' [. . . . U]RU-ŠE-^{1}dan-na-a a-na [. . .]
7' [. . . . DU]-u!-ni ⌈PAB 5⌉ SUḪUR
Rev 1' [IGI] $^{1.d!}$30-MAŠ LÚ-3-šú ⌈šá!⌉ L[Ú!-. . .]
10' [LÚ!-GA]R.KUR URU-BÀD-^{1}MAN-GI[N] (last line!)

ADD 378 (AR 429) Obv 7 i- [sign] -ra-šu [.(.)]
12 TA* IGI ^{1}DINGIR-ma-la-k[u]!
16-17 lost
Edge 18! l[u!-u . . . . .]
Rev 11 IGI ^{1}tu!-[. . .]
16 ITU-ŠE! [. . . . .] (U)

ADD 380 (AR 428) Obv 4 [ina]! URU-⌈ki⌉-si-⌈ri!⌉
5 SUḪUR ŠÀ.GA ⌈ša!⌉ ^{1}⌈15!⌉-DU-⌈IGI⌉
6 SUḪUR [[ ]] KASKAL [ša a-n]a [UR]U!- [signs] (U*)
7 i-la-ku!-u-ni (U)

ADD 382 (AR 395) Obv 1 (end) iš-k[un]
2 A LÚ-AZU ([signs]) sic
4 i-na ma-al-gu-te sic (signs clear)
6 É 8BÁN! A.ŠÀ (U)
8 sic
12 [. . . . . . .]-ra-a-te sic (U: -ti)
Rev 1' ⌈IGI ^{1}suk-ka-a-a ina IGI! IGI!-MEŠ! URU!⌉- [signs]
2' ^{1}PAB-u+a-a (written [signs])
5' followed by a blank space of about 4 lines
6' lim-mu ^{1}tak-lak-a-na-[^{d}]EN

ADD 384 (AR 436) Obv Beginning lost, then [n+]1 stamp seal impression[s]
!
1' $^{1.d}$IM-DÙ D[UMU! . . .]
2' É 15 ANŠE ŠE-NUM[UN . . . .]
3' ina ma-za-ru-te bu-⌈ra!-a!⌉-[te . . .]
5' 30! MA.N[A
6' a!-na! (sic) $^{1.d}$30-A-SUM-na LÚ- [sign]] (U)
8' kás!(not kas-)pu ga-mur
Edge 16' 
Rev 6 kás!-pu
7 ú-ta-a!-ra (U)
11 sic (signs clear)
12 IGI $^{1.d}$IM-MU-GAR [signs]
13 IGI ^{1}ub-ru-^{d} [sign]

ADD 385 (AR 194) Obv 2' a-na! ⌈$^{1!}$⌉[. . . . .] (U*)
!
3 stamp seal impressions

ADD 385 (AR 194)	Obv	5'	TA*!( ) IGI ^{1}EN-NÍG.GÁL-BÀD! LÚ*-SAG! A-MAN
		6'	TA*! IGI LÚ*!(not LÚ)-MEŠ
		11'	A.Š[À Š]a! $^{1.d}$PA-DUB-NUMUN
		13'	[ša ^{1}]AD-[DÙG]!.⌜GA!⌝ (spaced)
	Rev	1	SUḪUR KASKAL ša TA*! URU-kur-b[a-ìl]
		2	⌜ša!⌝ ⌜a-na⌝ URU-ana-tú
		3	PAB 1-⌜en⌝ BUR! SAG!+DU! É [. . .]
		5	TA*! IGI ^{1}am-me-ni-DINGIR ša! TA* IGI ^{1}AD-DÙG.GA (wr.)
		6	il-qi-u-nu SUḪUR KASKAL (wr.) URU-ana-tú
		7	(end) ^{1}AD-DÙG.GA ( )
		9	IGI ^{1}e( )-ṭè-ri IGI ^{1}šul-lum!-a!
		11	IGI ^{1}TUKU( )-ši-DINGIR
		12a	———————————————!
		13	IGI ^{1}ZALAG-e( )-a LÚ*-A.BA KUR-ár-ma-a-a šá ⌜A!⌝-MAN
		14	LÚ*-PAB( )-šú šá ^{1}EN-NÍG.GÁL-BÀD!( )
		15	[IGI ^{1}]m[an!-n]u!-ki!-^{d}PA : (U)
		16	[IGI . . . . .(.) ^{1}]ma[n-n]u-ki-ŠÀ-URU
ADD 386 (AR 171)	Obv		Beginning destroyed
			Seal space
			———————————————!
		1'	[É . ANŠE A.ŠÀ.G]A ina GIŠ-BÁN ša! 10! [qa . . .] (U)
		2'	[. . . .] ⌜ŠÀ!⌝ IGI+2-MEŠ ad!-ru!
		3'	[. . . . . . ša zu!(U)- -zu-na-pi
		6'	[. . . . Š]À! IGI+2-MEŠ pu-ṣe-e É ši!-qi!
		10'	A.ŠÀ.GA za-ri!-bi la-a-qi 0! (U)
		16'	TA written
		18'	ša AD-ni šu!-u 0!
	Rev	2	[. . . .] a bi at . .]
		6	sic
			———————————————
		7	IGI ^{1}ab-di-U.U!
		9	sic
		10	[IGI ^{1}]ḫal-la-[b]a-a
		12	[IGI ^{1}š]u!-ma!-a-a LÚ*-SAG
ADD 387 (AR 34)	Obv	1	[N]A$_{4}$-KIŠIB $^{1.d}$ . . . . .]
		3a	———————————————!
			3 stamp seal impressions
			———————————————!
		4	[É] 5 ANŠE A.ŠÀ.GA (U)
		6	[ina URU-Š]E!-^{1}ZÁLAG-É (U)
		7	[. . . . . .]

ADD 387 (AR 34)	Rev	1'	[IGI] ⌜^{1}⌝na!-ni-i
		3'	LÚ*-GAL-///
		4'	[IGI] ^{1}ḫar-U.U! DUMU.MÍ pir-su ⌜GA!⌝
		5'	sic
		14'	[LÚ-SUKK]AL! GAL-[u]
ADD 388 (AR 425)	Obv	1	NA$_4$-KIŠIB ^{1}na-pi-///]
		2	: ^{1}15-I NA$_4$-KIŠIB ^{1}ri!-[. . .]
		6a	————!
			three (identical) stamp seal impressions
			————!
		8	[SUHUR ma]š!-qi-i
		9	[SUHUR ^{1}]se!-da!-la!-///
		10	[. .]⌜x⌝ ḫa!-me! ///. . .]
	Rev	1'	[IG]I!⌜$^{1!.d!}$⌝[. . . . .]
			————!
		2'	IGI $^{1.d}$PA-PAB-AŠ
		9'	IGI ^{1}⌜na⌝-bi-si-ik-ki sic
ADD 389 (AR 170)	Obv	1'	[. . . . . . .(.)] ⌜da/ša an⌝[. . . .]
		2'	[. . . . ! ina ŠÀ]-bi GIŠ-BÁN ša ⌜10⌝ [qa]
		4'	[. . . . SUḪUR KAS]KAL+2! [ša a-na]! URU-ŠE-bir-[. . .]
		5'	⌜DU!⌝-[u-ni . . . S]UḪU[R] KASKAL+2! LUGAL ša URU-[. .]
		6'	ú!-[piš-ma ^{1}EN- . .]/// TA* IGI LÚ*-MEŠ-⌜e!⌝
		7'	šu-a-tú! i[l-q]i [ka]s-pu ga-mur [ta-din]
	Edge	9'	tu-a-ru de-⌜nu⌝ DUG$_4$.DUG$_4$ l[a!-áš-šú]
		10'	[ma]n-⌜nu⌝ ša ina ur-kiš ina ma!-⌜te!⌝-[ma GIL-u-ni]
	Rev	1	[lu]-u LÚ*-MEŠ-[e an]-nu-[te]
		3	(end) mim-ma-n[u!-šú-nu]
		11	[in]a de-e!-⌜ni⌝-[šú
	L.E.	2	ṣa-bit ṭup-pu!
ADD 391 (AR 394)	Obv	2	ṣu-pur ^{1}še-⌜er-ri!⌝-id-ri EN A.ŠÀ SUM-ni (U)
			————!
			unused space for fingernail impressions
			————!
		6	(end) ^{1}KUR!-URI-a-a
		14	[. . . .] É 1 ANŠE A.[ŠÀ . . . .]
		15	SUḪUR ^{1}qi-⌜bit⌝-[né-e
		16	⌜É⌝ 4BÁN GIŠ-GU.ZA /// . . . . .]
		17	[É]! 1 ANŠE BÁN A.ŠÀ ina URU-LÚ-[. . . .]!
		18	[. . .]-šá-É ú-piš-ma [$^{1.d}$MAŠ-DINGIR-a-a]!
		19	[TA*]! IGI ^{1}še-er-id-ri ina [. . . . .]

ADD 391 (AR 394) Edge 21-22 sic (U restores incorrectly)
Rev 12 [IGI] ^{1}aš-šur-nat-kil LÚ-GA[L!-. . .]
13 (end) LÚ-ḫa-z[a] a[n!-nu]

ADD 394 (AR 169) Obv 1' [. . . . ANŠ]E! A!.Š[À! SUḪUR ^{1}K]UR-URI-⌜a⌝-[a . . . . .]
2' [. . . .]! SUḪUR ^{1}[za-b]i-ni SUḪUR ^{1}EN-T[I]!
3' [. . . .  SUḪUR ^{1}[kan]-nun-a-a SUḪUR ^{1}EN-T[I]!
4' [. . . .]! SUḪUR AMA! ⌜šá!⌝ URU-ŠE-^{1}zi-z[i!-i]
5' [SUḪUR URU-LÚ-DUG.QA.B]UR!-MEŠ É 5 ANŠE A.ŠÀ SU[ḪUR . . .]
6' [. . SUḪUR ^{1}E]N!-TI! SUḪUR AMA šá URU-ŠE-^{1}[zi-zi-i]
7' [. . . . É n] ANŠE A.ŠÀ SUḪUR ^{1}qi-[bit-né-e]
8' [. . .(.) SUḪU]R KASKAL šá URU-kàl!-ḫa É! 4BÁ[N . . .]
9' [É 1 AN]ŠE BÁN A.ŠÀ šá MAN? šá! ina!  . . . .]
10' [. . . .  ina ma-⌜al⌝-[g]u-te [. . . . .] (sic)
11' [. . . .] É! [. ANŠ]E! A.ŠÀ [. . . . . .]!
12' [. . . . SUḪ]UR A.ŠÀ [. . . .]
13' [. . . . . .] AMA! ša! UR[U-ŠE . . .] (U)
14' [. . . . .] ⌜SUḪUR⌝ [. . . . .]
Rev 1'! [. . . . .  -i! u! DUMU
3'! [. MA.NA KUG.UD LUḪ-u . MA.N]A KUG.GI sak-ru ina! [bur-ki]
4'! [^{d}MAŠ a-šib URU-kal]!-ḫi GAR-an
5'! [. . . . . . . AN]ŠE-ḫar-bak-kan-ni
6'! (end) LÚ-E[N.NAM URU-šú!]
7'! [SUM-an kas-pu ana 10]-MEŠ-te ana EN-MEŠ-šú GUR.RA [0]
9'! [IGI ^{1}. .]-AŠ! LÚ-laḫ-ḫi-nu É-kad-mu-ri
11'! (end) ^{d}PA šá URU- 
12'! [IGI ^{1}  -DU LÚ-GAL-še-lap-pa-a-[a]
13'! [IGI ^{1}  -A-PAB
14'! [IGI ^{1}s]e!-e'-[. .] LÚ-šá-qur!-[bu-ti]

ADD 395 (AR 393) Obv 1 ku-um NA$_{4}$-⌜KIŠIB⌝-[šú-nu ṣu-pur-šú-nu iš-ku-nu]!
2 ṣu-pur ^{1}AD-  [. . .] (spaced)
3 ṣu-pur ^{1}AD-  . . .]

4 fingernail impresssions

5 [SU]ḪUR um(wr. DUB)-me ša URU-tu!()- .]
7 [SUḪ]UR A.ŠÀ šá ^{1}GÌR!+2!-[. . .]
8 [. . . .] ⌜LÚ*!⌝-tur-[tan . . . .]
Rev 2' [IGI $^{1.d}$P]A!-MU-PAB [. . .]
2 lines blank; date

ADD 397 (AR 422) Obv 2 [ṣu-pu]r ^{1}ma!-... .]
4 [ṣu]-pur ^{1}ḫa-a-A[N!-. .]
5 [PA]B 3 LÚ-MEŠ-e ⌜EN⌝ [A.ŠÀ SUM-ni]

4 fingernail impressions, evidently by different persons

6 É 9 ANŠE 3BÁN! A.ŠÀ tab-⌜ru⌝ GA[L!-u]
8 (end) ^{1}na!-ga-⌜a!⌝ [O] (U*)
9 (end) ^{1}gam!-bu-la-⌜a!⌝-[a] (wr.)
10 (end) ^{1}kab- .]
12 ú-piš-ma ^{1}ú!-⌜ku!⌝-[.(.)] (U*)
13 DUMU ^{1}ia-KIN- .]
14 [TA*] IGI ^{1}ma-⌜RI!⌝-[.]
15 [TA* IGI] ^{1}aš+šur-PAB-M[EŠ!-. .]
16 [TA* IGI]! ^{1}ha!-a!-⌜an⌝ [. . . .]
Rev 2' [. . . .] za!-⌜ar!⌝-[pu la-qi-u] (U*)
3' [tu-a-ru de]-en-nu DUG$_{4}$.D[UG$_{4}$! la-áš-šú]
4' [man-nu šá ina u]r!-kiš ina mat-[e-ma]
8' [kas]-pu ⌜a-na⌝ O! EN-MEŠ G[UR.RA]

9' IGI ^{1}DINGIR-im-me [O]!
10' IGI ^{1}ka-ku!-s[u]! (U)
11' URU-ša-^{1}bir-ta-⌜a!⌝-[a]
12' [IG]I! ^{1}ki-s[i?-. . .]
L.E. 1 [. . . . . . .] ku-um . . .]
2 [. . . . . . . -a LÚ*-[. .]!

ADD 398 (AR 421) Obv 1 [. . . . . . .(.)]! EN A.ŠÀ SUM-ni

cylinder seal impression

2 [. . . . . -ba-al ina URU-mi[r!-. . .]
3 [. . . .]-MAN!-PAB SUḪUR URU-la-ḫi- . .]
4 [. . . .] SUḪUR ḫa-li-di! [. .] (U)
5 [. . .(.) ^{1}]^{d}aš+šur-EN-LAL [O]
6 [. . . SUḪ]UR! ^{1}di-d[i]-⌜i!⌝ [. . .]
Rev 2' [IGI ^{1}]⌜sa!⌝-si-i [O]
3' [IGI $^{1.d}$M]AŠ!-i [O]
4' [IGI ^{1}. .]-⌜ú!⌝-tú! DUMU ^{1}ḫa-ri!-[. .] (U*)
5' [IGI ^{1}a!]-da!-la-la LÚ*-rak-sa [. . .] (sic, cf. r.6')
6' [IGI $^{1.d}$P]A!-sal-lim LÚ*-rak-sa ^{1}i[. .] ( )
7' [IGI ^{1}d]i!-di-i
9' [IGI ^{1}. -šu-šu
10' [IGI ^{1}.]-la!-bar-su! (U*)

ADD 400 (AR 396) Obv 2 sic
3a ———————————————!
two square stamp seal impressions
———————————————!
11 ú!-[p]iš-ma ^{1}[ku-k]u-la-nu (U*)
Rev 6 DUMU-DUMU-MEŠ-šú ub-[t]a-0!-u-ni
8 ú-GUR ina de-ni-šú D[U]G$_4$.D[UG$_4$-ma] (U)
9 (blank!) la i-la[q-qi]!
19 IGI ^{1}qar-ḫa-a 0! LÚ*-:

ADD 402 (AR 420) L.E.1 [. . . .]! ša A.ŠÀ šú-a-tú [. . . .]!
2 

ADD 403 (AR 419) Obv 1 NA$_4$-⌜KIŠIB⌝[
———————————!
1[+n] stamp seal impression[s]
———————————!
3 
Rev 2' IGI ^{1}di-U.U!-[. . .]
6' IGI ^{1}AŠ.PAB.[MEŠ 0!]
7' ina!(over erased IGI) tar-ṣi $^{1.d}$[. . .] (U)
L.E.1! [IGI ^{1}. . .]-bal-liṭ LÚ*-AB.BA sic

ADD 406 (AR 417) Obv 1' TA* IGI ^{1}ṣil-⌜aš+šur⌝-[DU]-⌜ak!⌝
7' lu-u ^{1}ṣil-aš+šur-DU 0!

ADD 408 (AR 415) Obv 4' [ú-piš-ma ^{1}rém-an-ni-^{d}IM LÚ-DIB-PA]!-MEŠ! dan!-nu
5' [. . . .] LÚ*-[. . . . . .] ki
8' A.ŠÀ za-ar-pi [laq-qi! man-nu] ša ina ur!-k[iš]! (U*)
10' sic (U omits ša)
Edge 12' ub-ta-'u-u-ni ka[s!-pu a-na 10-MEŠ-te]
13' [a-na E]N!-[MEŠ]-šú! [GUR]-ra
Rev 1 [ina de-ni-šú DUG$_4$]!.⌜DUG$_4$⌝-ma la ⌜i!⌝-laq-qi (U)
7 [IGI $^{1.d}$AMAR.UTU-M]U!-PAB LÚ-GAL-ḪAL
8 [IGI ^{1}ba-ni-i] LÚ!-2-u LÚ-GAL-A.ZU (U)
9 (end) É- . . .]
11 [IGI ^{1}. . . .  IGI ^{1}bu-di!-[b]a!-al!

ADD 409 (AR 453) Obv 1' [. . . . . .] nu [. . .]
2' [SUḪUR A].ŠÀ ^{1}si-[.]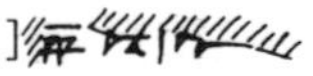
6' [. . .] É du!-gu-li!
8' [tab-r]i!-ú

ADD 409 (AR 453)	Rev 1	[TA* IGI ^{1} -te!-e il-qi (U)
	4	[. . . . NA$_{4}$-kan-nu [[tab!-ri!]]-ú!
ADD 415 (AR 438)	Obv 8	(end) LÚ-MEŠ-[e]! O!
	9	[an-nu-ti! EN A].ŠÀ-MEŠ
	Rev 1'	[. . . . . . .] LÚ*-qu[r!-bu-ti]
	2'	[IGI ^{1}. .]-u-a DUMU ^{1}ša-aš+šur!-⸢a!⸣-[..]
	6'	[IG]I $^{1.d}$MAŠ-⸢i!⸣
	7'	IGI ^{1}su-si-i[a LÚ*]-SIMUG-KUG.GI ša ⸢É⸣ LÚ*-[SUKKA]L! (U*)
ADD 416 (AR 438)	Obv 5	É : ad-ru me-šil! GIŠ-ŠAR (U)
	8	[SUḪUR] KASKAL! [ša] ⸢URU+ŠE!⸣ [. .]
	Rev 1'	⸢x x⸣[
		———————————————————————————!
	2'	IGI $^{1.d}$U.GUR-MAN-P[AB L]Ú*!(not LÚ)-SAG ša LÚ*!-GAL!-]
	4'	sic
	5'	LÚ*!-i-tu-'a-a-a
	7'	IGI ^{1}TA*!-^{d}IM-PAB-u-tú ÌR ša LÚ*!-SUKKAL
	11'	(end) URU-ni/sa-ḫu-ut-a-a
	12'	ṭup- written
ADD 417 (AR 449)	Obv 1'	[. . . . . . . t]a!-ad-⸢din!⸣ [O]! (U)
	2'	(end) šú-a-⸢tú!⸣ [za-ar-pu]!
	Rev 6	IGI ⸢^{1}⸣bu-la!-lu LÚ-A.ZU
ADD 418 (AR 211)	Obv	Beginning destroyed
		1[+n] stamp seal impression[s]
	3'	SUḪUR ÍD-⸢a⸣- SUḪUR ^{1}. . .]-SI.SÁ
	4'	SUḪUR ma-ú!-te ša [^{1}. . . . . .-n]i! (U*)
	5'	É 10 ANŠE A.⸢ŠÀ ša!⸣ DIN]GIR-a-a
	10'	ina URU-bur-ri-im URU-qa-di-né-e
	Edge 14'	TA*! (not TA) IGI ^{1}EN-MAN-PAB TA*!
	15'	TA*! IGI ^{1}aš+šur-ši-i (sic!)
	Rev 7-8	TA*! not TA
	11	(end) ú-⸢ta!⸣-r[a]!
	14	3+si+šú sic (wr.)
	19	[IGI ^{1}. . . . .]!-te
	20	[IGI ^{1}. . . . . IGI ^{1}]NUMUN-GIN
	23	[IGI ^{1}. . . . . LÚ-GIG]IR!-DU$_{8}$-MEŠ

ADD 419 (AR 444) Obv 1' [. . .] qi! [

2' 10 ANŠE A.ŠÀ ⸢1!⸣ GIŠ-SAR GIŠ!-[til-lit . . . . .]

3' [. . . . .]! URU-ŠE-dan!-a-⸢a⸣ [. . . . .]⸢x x⸣

4' [. . . . URU-Š]E-1!-zu!-um!-bi [. . . . .] ri-pi-tú

5' [. . . .]! ina URU-^{d}UTU-ri-qa

6' ⸢GIŠ!-til!-lit!⸣ 6 GIŠ-SAR-MEŠ ⸢ši!⸣-qi A-MEŠ É!-MEŠ! ina na-gi-i KUR-arrap-ḫa

7' [š]a $^{1.d}$⸢AMAR.UTU-SU ša⸣ ^{1}SU-PAB-MEŠ ša! ^{1}GIN!-i! ina URU-⸢^{d}⸣UTU-r[i-qa] (U)

8' ú-piš-ma ⸢^{1}rém-a-ni⸣-^{d}IM LÚ*-mu-kil!-KUŠ-[PA-MEŠ dan-nu]

9' [š]a ^{1}⸢aš+šur⸣-DÙ-⸢DUMU⸣.UŠ LUGAL KUR-aš+šur-KI ina Š[À . . . . . .]

10' [(.). . š]a e-gír-ra-MEŠ-te TA*! [. . . . .]

11' [. ^{1}rém]-a-ni-^{d}IM LÚ*-[. . . . .]

Rev 1 [i]l-⸢qi⸣ kas-pu ga-mur ta-din-ni A.ŠÀ-MEŠ ⸢É!⸣-[MEŠ . . . . .]

4 (end) lu-u ^{1}GIN-i DUMU ^{1}S[U!-PAB-MEŠ]

ADD 420 (AR 100) Obv 3' URU-DUL-na-ḫi-ri sic

4' (end) ^{1}e!-ni-D[INGIR]

5' (end) ŠEŠ-š[ú]!

6' ^{MÍ}pa-pa!-a

7' (end) É ri-pi-t[ú]!

10' [ša] $^{1!}$aš+šur-DÙ-A LUGAL KUR-aš+šur-K[I]!

14' [kas]-pu gam-mur ta-ad-[di]n!

15' (end) šu-⸢a⸣-[tu]

16' [za-a]r-pu [. . . .]

Rev 1' [IGI ^{1}]PAB-la-maš-ši L[Ú!-3.U$_{5}$]

4' (end) LÚ!(not LÚ*)-GIŠ.G[IGIR-DU$_{8}$-MEŠ]

5' IGI ^{1}se-e'-DIL.AM :! (not ⁝) [0]

6' (end) :! [0]

7' IGI $^{1.d}$15-SUM!(not AŠ)-A LÚ!-A.BA [ṣa-bit dan-ni-te]

ADD 421 (AR 100a) Obv 1 [NA$_{4}$-KIŠIB] $^{1.d}$nu-uš-ḫu-sa-lìḫ!-an-ni (U)

5 URU-DUL-na-ḫi-ri sic

6 [. . . . .(.)! ^{1}qar-ḫ]a-a L[Ú*!-ENGAR ^{1}e-ni-DINGIR]

7 [0! ^{1}ab-šá-a Š]EŠ-šú ^{MÍ}p[a-pa-a AMA-šú-nu]

Rev 1 [ina de-ni]-šú! DU[G!.DUG$_{4}$-ma . . .]

14 [IGI $^{1.d}$15-SU]M!-A

ADD 422 (AR 103) Obv 2 [E]N A.ŠÀ É UN-MEŠ S[UM!-ni]

———————————————!

3 fingernail impressions

———————————————!

ADD 422 (AR 103) Obv 3 [É] ⌜50!⌝ ANŠE A.ŠÀ 10 lim GIŠ-⌜til-lit⌝ (U)
4 [É e]p-šú ^{1}ha-šá-na! 4 DUMU-MEŠ-šú (U)
6 DUMU.[MÍ-sa P]AB 9! ZI-MEŠ ÌR-⌜MEŠ⌝(U)
9 TA* [IGI ^{1}b]ar-ḫa-te, ina ŠÀ-bi; cf. r.3
13 za-a[r-pu laq-qi-u]
Rev 1 tu-a-ru de-e-nu ⌜da!⌝-b[a!-bu la-áš-šú] (U*)
2 man-nu ša ina ur-kiš ⌜GIL⌝-[u-ni]
3 lu ^{1}bar-ḫa-te ⌜lu!⌝ DUMU-MEŠ-šú
6 ⌜de⌝-e-nu da-ba-bu ⌜ub⌝-t[a-u]-⌜ni!⌝ (U)
7 [. MA].NA KUG.⌜UD 1 MA⌝.NA KUG.GI s[ak!-r]u! (U)
8 [ina bur-k]i! ^{d}iš-tar a-ši-bat ⌜URU⌝-[NINA] ⌜GAR!-an!⌝
9 [kas-pu] ⌜a⌝-na 10-MEŠ a-[na] EN-šú ⌜GUR⌝ [O]
11 [IGI ^{1}.-D]UMU!-ZÁLAG
12 [IGI ^{1}. .]!-^{d}PA LÚ*!- -ru! ⁝!
13 [IGI ^{1}. .]!-qa!-mu O! LÚ*-mu-⌜kil⌝-PA-MEŠ ⁝
14 [IGI ^{1}.]-⌜mu!⌝-za- IGI] ^{1}ra-p[a-i]a

ADD 423 (AR 104) Obv 1' ⌜ÌR-MEŠ ^{1}bar⌝-ḫ[a-te . . . .(.)]
4' TA* IGI ^{1}bar-te-[. .(.)] sic
Edge 13' lu-u ^{1}bar-ḫa-a[t! .(.)]
15' lu-u qur-ub!-[šú O]
Rev 2 šá TA* ^{1}šúm-m[u-DINGIR-MEŠ-ni (DUMU-MEŠ-šú)]
9 ⌜ina de-ni-šú DUG$_4$!⌝.[DUG$_4$-ma]

ADD 424 (AR 90) Obv 2' 2!
4' ^{1}⌜šá!-^{d}!⌝[
6' ^{1}ba-n[i!-i (U)
7' ^{1}APIN!-ka-
10' PAB 5 ZI-MEŠ O! (line spaced out)
Rev 2 (end) ša MAN KUR(over erased aš+šur)-aš+šur
3 ina ŠÀ 30! sic (U incorrectly 40)
4 A.ŠÀ-MEŠ É-MEŠ UN-MEŠ il!-qi! kas!-pu (U)
6 [. . . . . tu]-a-ru! (U)
8 [. . . . .]-ban!-ni!
9 [. . . . .]-šú!
10 [. . . . .]-ni!
11 [. . . . .]-⌜ru!⌝
L.E.! 1 [. . . .(.)]x[
2 [. . . .(.)]⌜su⌝[

ADD 424 (AR 90) L.E.3 [IGI ^{1}ÌR-n]a-na!-a ⸢LÚ*⸣-[

ADD 425 (AR 413) Obv <u>Beginning destroyed; then unused space for seal impressions</u> !

1' É 2 ANŠE [A.ŠÀ] ⸢SUḪUR!⸣ ^{1}man-nu-ki-i-arba-ìl-KI

2' LÚ-GIŠ.GIGIR [SUḪUR O!] ÍD 1 ANŠE 4BÁN

3' SUḪUR ^{1}PAB- . .] ⸢É!⸣ 8BÁN SUḪUR ^{1}man-nu-ki-PAB-M[EŠ]

4' SUḪUR ⸢É!⸣ [^{1}. .]-ma-ti-te! É 2BÁN

5' SU[ḪUR . . . . n]a-ḫal sic

8' [É] 1 ANŠE 5BÁN :! ^{1}PAB-qa-⸢mu!⸣ [. . . . .]

9' (end) ^{MÍ}sa-⸢ma!⸣-[. . .]

11' É 7! ANŠE A.ŠÀ URU- $^{1.d}$EN.ZU!-KAR!-ir! (U)

18' (end) É 5 [ANŠE] O!

Rev 1 PAB É 40! A.ŠÀ . . . .]

4 ^{1}DINGIR!-⸢DIB!⸣-an-ni ⸢LÚ!-SAG⸣ MAN ina ŠÀ-[bi]

7 de-e-nu DUG$_4$.DUG$_4$ O! man-nu (sic!)

8 GIL-ú!(not U)-ni

13 (end) ⸢LÚ-GAL⸣-ki-ṣi[r O?]

14 IGI ^{1}ḫa-ba-áš-t[i LÚ-G]AL-Ì.DU$_8$-[MEŠ]

15 sic

16 (end) -KUŠ-⸢PA⸣-[MEŠ šá A-MAN]

19 (end) LÚ-⸢ša!-IGI!⸣-[. .]

ADD 426 (AR 89) Obv 1' [. . . . . DUMU].MÍ-su

2' [. . . . .]-DINGIR DUMU-šú GA!

3' [. . . . . . -ṣi! DUMU.MÍ-su 4 ru!-ṭ[u]! (U)

4' [. . . . .]!-⸢a!⸣-te! ^{1}ag-du-ud pir GA [O] (sic!)

6' [. . . AN]ŠE! 8BÁN! 8 ½ qa

7' [. . . .] -en-ḫu ú-piš-ma ^{1}lu-TI.⸢LA!⸣

Edge 8' [LÚ-. .] ša ^{1}DI-^{d}MAŠ LÚ-EN.NAM . . .]

9' [. . .]-BAR ina ŠÀ DIL GÚ+UN ⸢AN!.BAR!⸣ [. . . . .]

10' (end) É ⸢A!.⸣ŠÀ GIŠ!-[SAR UN-MEŠ]

11' (end) ⸢de-e⸣-[nu DUG$_4$.DUG$_4$]!

Rev 6 [. . . . .! de]-e-nu

8 [. . . . . NA$_4$-ZA.GÌN ḫi-ip (cf ADD 498:10'!)

ADD 427 (AR 186) Obv 6 ina URU-uš-ḫi-O!-ri-ti (U)

8 (end) LÚ*-ENGAR MAN!

10 ⸢ú⸣-piš-m[a ^{1}šum-ma-DINGI]R-⸢MEŠ⸣-ni

17 ina ma-te-e!-me (U)

ADD 427 (AR 186) Rev 2 ša TA*! (not TA)

3 TA*! DUMU-MEŠ-šú

7 [IGI ^{1}s]a-ma-a' LÚ*-mu-⌜rib!⌝-[ba-n]u [ša]! ⌜DUMU!-MAN!⌝

8 (end) LÚ*-GUR!-UM[UŠ]!

10 ša ⌜GIŠ⌝-ut-tar-MEŠ (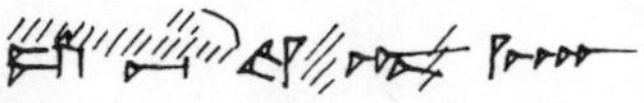)

16 ITU-DU$_{6}$! (not DUL)

17 dim wr. 

ADD 429 (AR 105) Obv 1 [N]A$_{4}$-⌜KIŠIB⌝ [^{1}. . .]! ^{1}GIN-AD!-u-a A-šú

2 [PA]B! 2! LÚ-[. . .]-a-a EN A.ŠÀ.GA

3 É ši!-q[i! . . .] ta-da-ni

---!

4 stamp seal impressions

---!

4 [. . . . . . .(.)] SUḪUR A.ŠÀ ša ^{1}GÌR+2!-15 (U)

7 (end) 6! ANŠE

12 [. . . . . . .(.)] qi! [. . . .]!

13 [. . . . . . .(.)] ṣi! nu u [. .]!(U*)

18 (end) a-na URU]-ḫi-li DU-u-ni

19 [. . . . . . . ^{1}.]-⌜su!⌝-u-a LÚ*-A.BA

21 [. . . . . . .] ⌜É!⌝ 22! ANŠE A.ŠÀ.GA (U*)

26 [. . . . .] : ^{1}bi-e!-lu!-ḫa-lu-ṣu

Edge uninscribed (nothing missing!)

Rev 1 [. . . . . PA]B-ma [. . . . . . .]!

2 [ú-piš-ma ^{1}rém-an-ni-^{d}IM LÚ*]-mu!-kil-[KUŠ-PA-MEŠ]

3 [dan-nu šá ^{1}aš+šur-DÙ-A MAN KUR]-aš+šur! [ina ŠÀ-bi]

4 [. . . . . . .(.) KUG].⌜UD!⌝ ša! URU!-[gar-ga-mis]!

5 [TA* IGI ^{1}. . . ^{1}GIN]-AD!-u-a [il-qi]

6 [kas-pu ga-mur ta-din]-ni A.ŠÀ.GA GIŠ-[SAR]

10 [GIL-u-ni lu ^{1}. . . ^{1}GIN-A]D!-u-a DUMU-MEŠ-šú-nu

14 [DUG$_{4}$.DUG$_{4}$ ub-ta-u-ni ANŠE-KUR.RA BA]BBAR! ina GÌR+2

17 [. . . . .] be-ni

25 [IGI] ^{1}[. . . . . . . LÚ*]-GAL- SAG!

26 IGI ^{1}PAB-⌜la⌝-[maš-ši] LÚ*-:

27 IGI $^{1.d}$šú-la!-[. . . .] 0!

28 IGI ^{1}am-me-n[i!-. . .] LÚ*-:

29 IGI ^{1}bi-bi!-[. . . .] LÚ*-:

31 [IG]I ^{1}gam-[. . . LÚ*-qur-b]u!-te

32 [IGI ^{1}]$^{.d!}$P[A!- . . . . . .]-MEŠ

NB: the three fragments constituting this tablet have not been physically joined together and are kept in separate boxes

ADD 430 (AR 32) Obv 2 DUMU ^{1}ib- [illegible] -ia
4 É 20 ANŠE A.ŠÀ ú!-gar!-ru
6 bur! $^{1.d}$PA-SIG$_5$ MÍ-su-šú!
Rev 1' IGI ^{1}⌜a!⌝-[. . .]
2' IGI $^{1.}$⌜^{d}PA⌝-[. . .]
3' IGI ^{1}⌜la!⌝-[. . .]
two lines uninscribed; date

ADD 431 (AR 98) Obv 2 <u>EN [A.ŠÀ-MEŠ] ⌜É!⌝-MEŠ GIŠ-SAR-MEŠ UN-MEŠ</u> ta-da-ni
——————————————— !
cylinder seal impression
Rev 10' IGI ^{1}ḫa-am[. . . . .] MAN!
12' IGI $^{1.d}$PA-KA[R!-. . . . . .] (U)
13' IGI $^{1.d}$PA-še-zib [. . . . . URU-a]rrap!-ḫa! (U)
15' ITU-BA[RAG! UD-.-K]AM! lim-[mu ^{1}i]t!-ri-DINGIR
16' L[Ú*-GAR.K]UR URU-la-ḫ[i-ri] (U)

ADD 432 (AR 107) Obv nothing missing at the beginning (!)
1 [. . . . . .] [illegible] EN A.ŠÀ-MEŠ GIŠ-SAR-MEŠ UN!-MEŠ! SUM-ni (U*)
——————————————— !
unused space for stamp seal impressions
——————————————— !
3 [. . . . . ina m]a-za-ru-te ÍD A-MEŠ ka-a-a-ma!-nu! (U)
4 [. . . . .] KA!-šá iz-zak-ru (U)
5 [. . . . .]-la!-a LÚ-GIŠ-APIN
6 (end) [illegible] ZI-MEŠ
7 [. . . . . [illegible] -SU! PAB 5! ZI-MEŠ
Rev 8 [lim-mu ^{1}gi-ḫi-lu] LÚ-GAR.KUR
9 [0 URU-ḫa-ta-r]ik!-ka

ADD 433 (AR 108) Obv 1' ⌜EN⌝ UN-MEŠ A.⌜ŠÀ⌝ GIŠ-S[AR-MEŠ ta-da-ni]
——————————————— !
cylinder seal impression (!)
——————————————— !
3' sic
4' (end) SUḪUR Í[D!-. .]
6' [SUḪUR ÍD]-⌜i!⌝-lab-bi-a-šú
8' [(.). . . . [illegible] 1-a-a- [illegible]. . .]
Rev 1'! [kas-pu a-na 10-M]EŠ!-⌜te! a!⌝-[na EN-šú GUR.RA]
2'! [ina de-ni-šú]! DUG$_4$.DUG$_4$-ma [. . .]
———————————————
3'! [IGI $^{1.d}$MAŠ!].MAŠ-MAN-PAB sic (against Ungnad)
11'! (end) LÚ*-ḫa-za-[nu . . . .]!

ADD 434 (AR 54) Obv 1' [É] 1 ANŠE ⸢SUḪUR⸣ [. . . . .]

2' SUḪUR KASKAL URU-ṣal-li-ib!-ši ⸢SUḪUR⸣ $^{1!}$. . . . .]

3' (end) ša URU-É!-. .(.)]

4' (end) É-⸢ku⸣-ti-⸢i!⸣ [.(..)]

6' KASKAL URU-É-ku-ti-i [SUḪUR ^{1}. .-b]a!-⸢ni!⸣

7' sic

8' É 1 ANŠE 2BÁN SUḪUR ^{1}DIN[GIR-... SUḪUR ^{1}]ḫa-na-si

9' (end) SUḪUR ^{1}[. . .]-⸢ba!⸣-ni

10' [SUḪUR ^{1}]·⸢^{d}UTU⸣-iq-bi SUḪUR AMA URU-DUL(sic)-LÚ*-KUR.GAR.RA

Edge 11' [SUḪUR . . .]-ni É 1! ANŠE! 6BÁN A.ŠÀ

12' [. . . . . . .]-⸢ku!⸣ SUḪUR um-me (U)

Rev 1 [. . . . . PA]B! 23! ANŠE A.ŠÀ

5 (end) 6 MA .NA 4!-tú! LAL!

6 [KUG.UD! ina 1 MA.N]A! ša LÚ*-DAM.QAR il-⸢qi!⸣(U*)

8 [pu-ṣe-e 0! t]a-din tu-a-ru de-en-nu DU[G$_4$.DU]G$_4$! [l]a-šú!

9 [man-nu š]a! ina ur-kiš ina ma-ti-ma lu-u! ^{1}KAR-ir-[^{d}KU]

10 (end) ša de-en-n[u DUG$_4$.DUG$_4$!]

11 [TA* ^{1}zi-zi]-⸢i!⸣ub-ta-u-ni ka[s-pu . . . . . .]

ADD 435 (AR 447) Obv 2a two oval stamp seal impressions; no rulings

4 1-en b[u!-ru

5 SUḪU[R!

6 : KASKAL+⸢2!⸣ [(U)

7 : ia!-[ar-ḫi (U)

10 gab-di AMA š[á!

Edge 14 PAB 40 ANŠE A.ŠÀ 2! ⸢É!⸣-[MEŠ . .]

Rev 5 LÚ*-GAL-S[AG!

6 TA*!(not TA) ^{1}SA[NGA!- (; A[L / LA[G also possible)

8 A.ŠÀ-MEŠ É-⸢MEŠ⸣ . .]

L.E. 2 LÚ*-GIŠ.BAN!.TAG.GA

ADD 436 (AR 163) Obv 1'! [. . . ^{1}man-nu]-ki!-i-aš+[šur . . . . . .(.)]

2'! [. . .]-ri ú-p[iš!-ma ^{1}A-a-a]

7'! [man-nu šá ina m]a-te-e-ma ina EGIR-at (sic; cf. U)

9'! [lu-u ^{1}man-nu]!-ki-i-aš+šur lu-u ^{1}li-i'-ti-ru-u (sic)

10'! [lu-u ^{1}.]-ru-ku-[. .]! lu-u DUMU-MEŠ-šú-nu (U*)

12'! l[u!-u DUMU-PAB]-MEŠ-šú-nu l[u!-u mam]-ma!

Rev 3 ⸢i⸣-qab-bu-u-ni ma-a kas-pu la! gam-mur (U)

8 GAL-te TA* 2BÁN ÚŠ-ERIN a-na be-lit-$^{d!}$EDIN (U)

9 (end) a-na ⸢10!⸣-[T]A!-a-a

10 (end) ina d[e!-ni-šú]

ADD 436 (AR 163) Rev 11 DUG$_4$.DUG$_4$-ma la T[I!-qi]
13 IGI ^{1}[n]a!-ḫa[r-. . . . . . .]

ADD 437 (AR 440) Obv 2 [EN] ⌜É!⌝ A.ŠÀ GIŠ-SA[R] (U)
3 [. . . . .] šá Ú-SAR [SUM-n]i!
———————————— !
2[+n] stamp seal impressions
———————————— !
4 [É ep]-šú a-di [. . . . .]
Balance of Obverse lost
Rev 1'![ina de-ni-šú] ⌜DUG$_4$!⌝[DUG-ma . . .]
————————————
2' [IGI ^{1}. . .]-la IGI ^{1}[. . . . .]
3' [IGI ^{1}. .] -a-a IGI
4' [IGI ^{1}. . .] IGI ^{1}
5' [IGI ^{1}. . . . .]-⌜DÙ⌝ IGI ^{1}[DINGIR-m]a!-a-di

ADD 438 (AR 132) Obv 4a impression of a square stamp seal; preceded but <u>not</u> followed by a dividing line
7! [. . . . .]! za-ku-u
Rev 1' [. . . . .]
one line uninscribed
2' [IGI ^{1}. . .]-šú GIŠ.GIGIR
4' [IGI ^{1}. . .]-i LÚ*-NAR! (U)
9' [IGI ^{1}. . . L]Ú*!-3.U$_5$
10' [IGI ^{1}. . . L]Ú*!-MA.LAḪ$_4$
Edge 12' [IGI ^{1}. . . G]AL!-TIN!
13' [IGI ^{1}. . . . .] IGI ^{1}ḫa-na!-na!

ADD 439 (AR 110) Obv 1 [NA$_4$-KIŠIB ^{1}]GIN!-a-ni-^{d}15 LÚ*-[. . .]
2 [UR]U!-qat!-ta-na-a-a EN A.ŠÀ.GA U[N-MEŠ]
3 [t]a- da- [ni]
———————————— !
4 stamp seal impressions
———————————— !
4 [E . ANŠE A].ŠÀ.G[A S]UḪUR ⌜KASKAL ša⌝ URU-ŠE-^{1}[. . .]
5 a!-na! [. . . . . il]-lak-u-ni SUḪUR [. . . .]
6 x[. . . . . . .] SUḪUR A.ŠÀ ša ^{1}SUM-ni-[. .] (sic; cf. U)
7 [. . . . .]! URU-ŠE-^{1}dan-na-a-[a]
8 [. . . . .] u [. . . .]!
9 [. . . . .] KASKAL! ša! ⌜a!-na!⌝[. .]
Rev 2' IGI $^{1.d}$[. . . . . .] a [. . . . .]!
3' IGI ^{1}NUMUN-u-t[i-i L]Ú*-mu-[kil-KUŠ-PA-MEŠ]

ADD 439 (AR 110) Rev 4' IGI $^{1.d}$30-[. . . L]Ú-S[A]G [. . . .]!

6' [IGI ^{1}].^{d}PA-SU LÚ*-2-u G[AL!-u-rat]

8' [IGI] ^{1}ba-ni-i LÚ*-⌜2!⌝-[u GAL-A.ZU]

9' [IGI ^{1}].$^{d!}$za!-⌜ba$_4$!⌝-[ba$_4$-SU . . . .]

ADD 440 (AR 151) Obv 1 [NA$_4$-KIŠI]B! ^{1}lu-ki-ma-ma (sic)

2 [NA$_4$-KIŠ]IB! ^{1}NUMUN-SI.SÁ

cylinder seal impression, no rulings

3 [EN A.ŠÀ!-M]EŠ UN-MEŠ SUM-nu (sic)

———————————————————!

4 [E . ANŠE] A.ŠÀ.GA-MEŠ

5 [. . . . l]u!-ub-la 0!

6 [. . . . . . a]n!-ni-ia!

7 [. . . . . .]⫽ A.GÀR-MEŠ

8 [. . . . . . L]Ú*-ENGAR

10 [ina ŠÀ . . . . .] ina! šá M[AN]!

11 [. . . . . ta]-⌜ad!⌝-[din]

Rev 1' [. . . . .-M]EŠ! D[UMU!-. .]

9' [IGI ^{1}. .]⫽-ši-i (spaced)

10' [IGI ^{1}]!-⌜DINGIR!⌝-[p]a!-a!-di

12' [IGI ^{1}s]u!-ra-ra-a-te

ADD 442 (AR 412) Obv Beginning destroyed

———————————————————!

1[+n] fingernail impression

———————————————————!

1' [. . .] ⌜A⌝.ŠÀ.GA-MEŠ šá [. . .]

2' [. . . .] SUḪUR SAG! A.Š[À! . . .]

3' [. . . .]-⌜a⌝-ni ú-piš (sic) $^{1.}$⌜d⌝-[. . .]

4' [. .]! ina ŠÀ-bi ½ MA.NA 5! G[ÍN! . . .]

5' [il-q]i! kas-pu TIL-mur A.ŠÀ.G[A šu-a-tú]

6' [T]A*! EN!-šú! la-qi t[u-a-ru]

ADD 443 (AR 97) Obv 2 sic

———————————————————!

unused space for stamp seal impressions

———————————————————!

4 [šá TA*]! URU-ma-li-ia-ti

5 [a-na UR]U-

7 [a]-na URU-ŠE-^{1}⫽⫽ DU-ku-u-ni

11 [ka]q-qi-r[i p]u-ṣe-e ina URU-[. . .]

12 ⌜^{1}tar⌝-ḫu-⫽-pi-i L[Ú-. . . .]

Rev 7' [IGI ^{1}. .]-⌜i!⌝ DUMU ^{1}[. . . .]

13' [IGI ^{1}. . .]-aṣ-bat! LÚ-Ì.⌜DU$_8$⌝ (U)

ADD 447 (AR 61) Obv 1 sic, very clear script
15 [il-qi kas-pu gam]-mur O!
16 [ta-din! UN-MEŠ GIŠ]-SAR-MEŠ O!
17 [. . . . . .] tu-a-ru di-i-[nu] O!
last line of Obverse destroyed
Rev 1! [. . . . .]
2! [. . . . . .] ma! [. . . . .]
3! [. . . . n]i! di-i-n[u]! O!
4! ⌜DUG$_{4}$.DUG$_{4}$⌝ TA* MÍ-šá-kín-te
17! MAN KUR aš+šur-KI lim-me ^{1}man-nu-ki-10-MAN! ( )

ADD 448 (AR 443) Obv 1 [NA$_{4}$]-KIŠIB ^{1}ba-ri-ki LÚ-GA[L-. .]
2 NA$_{4}$-KIŠIB ^{1}a-ba-il O! [. .]!
3a ———————————————!
unused space for stamp seal impressions
———————————————!
4 1 GIŠ-SAR lim GIŠ!-til!-lit! (sup.ras) [. . . . .] (U*)
5 (end) šá ^{1} [. . . . .]
6 2-u GIŠ-SAR ⌜2!⌝ [1]i[m! . . . .]
7 entirely obliterated
8 [3-su] GIŠ-SAR [O] 3! l[im! . . . .]
9 [šá ^{1}b]a!-al!-su!-ri x[. . . .]
10 [šu]-⌜u!⌝ DUMU-šú! DUMU.MÍ-su ^{1} . . . .]
12 GIŠ-til-lit-MEŠ 4/šá NA$_{4}$-i!-ga-[. . . . .] (U)
13 ina! KUR!-i-za-li š[á]! ^{1}ba-ri-k[i . . . . . .]
14 ina URU-is-pal-lu-r[e!-e . . . . .]
15 ú-piš-ma ^{1}rém-an-ni-⌜d⌝[IM LÚ-DIB-KUŠ-PA-MEŠ]
18 TI-qí! kas-pu gam-mur sic (cf. U)
19 É-MEŠ NA$_{4}$-i!-ga-r[u! . . . . . .] (U)
22 lu-u ^{1}ba-ri-ki l[u-u ^{1}a-ba-il]
Rev 1 lu-u LÚ-EN.NA[M!-su-nu . . . . .]
2 lu-u mim-ma-nu-šú-nu š[á! TA* (U)
3 (end) de!-[nu DUG$_{4}$.DUG$_{4}$]
5 (end) ^{d}iš-t[ar! a-ši-bat]
9 (end) LÚ-3-šu [. .]!
10 IGI ^{1}sa-si-i LÚ-ḫa-za-nu UR[U!-. .] (U*)
11 (end) LÚ-GAL-⌜A!⌝.[BA]
13 [IGI ^{1}M]U!-a-a DUMU $^{1.}$⌜d!⌝[. . . . .]
14 [IGI $^{1.d}$PA-SU]M!-MU LÚ-[. . . .] (SU]M =)
15 entirely obliterated
Edge 26 [IGI ^{1}. .]-⌜d!⌝IM L[Ú-. . . . .]
27 [IGI $^{1.d}$PA-r]i-iḫ-tú-PAB [O?]

ADD 453 (AR 187)	Obv 4	[. .! É ši]-qi
	5	[. . . .] ^{1}mil-ki-su!-[ri] (U)
	6	[. . . . .]-⸢a!⸣ MÍ-šú [0]
	8	[... ^{MÍ}UR]U!-NINA!-KI!-⸢i!⸣-[tú]
	10	[. . . . .]-šá-lip!-ḫur M[Í!-šú]
	Rev 4'	[GIL-u-ni . MA].NA KUG.UD 4! MA.[NA KUG.GI]
	5'	[. . . . . . . UR]U!-NINA SUM-an [0]
ADD 455 (AR 381)	Obv	Beginning lost, then what appears to be seal space
	1'!	[. . . . .] ⸢x x⸣ [. . .]
	2'!	[. . . . .] DUMU-šú x[. . .]!
	3'!	[. . . .] ⸢GA!⸣ PAB ⸢6⸣ ZI-[MEŠ ÌR-MEŠ]
	4'!	[^{1}.]-bi-⸢da!⸣-[. . . . .]
	5'!	[.] lim 6! me! GIŠ!-ṭ[il!-lit . . .] (U*)
	6'!	[P]Ú ina ŠÀ-bi URU!-[. . . . .]
	7'!	ú-piš-ma $^{1.}$⸢d!⸣[. . . .]
	Rev 1	[a-n]a! [10]-MEŠ!-⸢te!⸣ [. . . . .]
	2	[ina de]!-ni-šú DUG$_4$.D[UG$_4$-ma . . .]
	3	[IGI ^{1}]mu-na!-si- . . . . .]
	7	IGI ^{1}EN-⸢mu!⸣-[.(.) L]Ú*!-GIŠ.GIGIR qur!-bu!-[ti]
	9	sic
	10	[IGI ^{1}.]-ri-i- 0!
	11	[IGI ^{1}.]x-la! URU-a-mu!-x[. .]
		traces of 3 more lines, probably names of witnesses
ADD 457 (AR 78)	Obv 2'	sic
	3'	[. . . .]-MAN! DUMU!.MÍ-sa
	6'	[. . . . i]l!-qí kas!-⸢pu!⸣
	7'	[gam-mur ta-din UN-MEŠ šú-a-t]ú! ⸢zar!⸣-[pu]
	Edge	obliterated
	Rev	entirely destroyed
ADD 458 (AR 352)	Obv 1'	[. . . . .]
	3'	(end) ..] PAB 4! [0]
	4'	(end) ..]-man-nu-la-EN [0]
	5'	[. . . . .] qur! PAB 5 ZI-MEŠ
	9'	[. . . . .]-MEŠ 0!

ADD 460 (AR 199) Obv 1' [É . ANŠ]E! ⌜A!⌝.[ŠÀ ina UR]U!-⌜ka!⌝-a[n!-nu-u']
2' [SU]ḪUR um-me š[a] URU-ka-an-nu!-[u']
3' SUḪUR KASKAL ša a-na [UR]U-nu-⌜ḫu!⌝-bi D[U-u-ni] (U)
5' SUḪUR GIŠ-SAR ša [.(.).] a-ši-di
6' PAB!-ma! 40! A.ŠÀ . .
7' [
Rev 1' 10 MA.NA KUG.UD [. MA].⌜NA!⌝ [KUG.GI . . .]
2' ina ^{d}iš-tar a-ši-pat! URU-ni-nu-a . .] (U)
3' (end) EN-MEŠ-šú ú!-GU[R] (U)
5' de-e-šú! (U)

6' [IG]I ^{1}a[r!-. .] -zu! LÚ*-GAL-ki-ṣ[ir]
7' [IGI ^{1}. . . .]⌜x⌝ LÚ*-Ì.DU$_8$-M[EŠ]
8' [IGI ^{1}. . . . . . .]-⌜GAL-ki⌝-ṣ[ir]

ADD 461 probably letter or administrative memorandum
Obv 1' [. . . . .] a [. . . .]!
2' [. . . . . A].ŠÀ-šú a-na! A.ŠÀ . . .]
3' [. . . . A].⌜ŠÀ!⌝-šú ina UGU ANŠE-A.A[B!.BA]
4' [. . . . .]-ru! ina! KÚ! ša UN [MEŠ . .]
5' [. . . .]⌜ú!⌝-sa-aḫ-ḫa-ru-ni [. . .]
6' [. . . . .] -ri-⌜da!⌝-an!-ni!
8' [. . . . .]-ib!
Rev beginning destroyed; 5 lines blank
1' [PAP!-šú DUMU-AD-šú LÚ-qe-e-pu
2' [. .]-ki! is-si!-šú la u-da
about 5 lines blank

ADD 462 (AR 373) Obv 2' 4 MÍ.GUR[UŠ!-MEŠ
7' a-na ^{1}ka[b!-
9' ^{1}ḫal-di-
11' [i]l!-⌜qi!⌝ [
Rev 3 la i-l[a!-qi] (spaced)
7 IGI ^{1}e-z[i!-
L.E. 1 [. . . . . L]Ú*!-A.BA!
3 [. . . .] IGI ^{1}ḫal-mu-su L[Ú-. . . .]!

ADD 463 (AR 193) Obv Beginning lost; 2[+n] stamp seal impressions
!
1' [. . .] til-li-te
2' [. . . .] . . .] ki!
break of 2(!) lines (U)

ADD 463 (AR 193) Obv 8! LÚ*-mu-⌜tir!⌝-ṭè-me (U)
Edge 9! [š]a $^{1.d}$U+GUR-MU!-DÙ
Rev 2 [. . . .] 8 ANŠE . .]
3 [. . . . šá]-par-ti! K[Ú! . . .]
4 [man-nu ša . . U]D!-MEŠ DU-⌜u!⌝-[ni]
7 [IGI ^{1}. . .] URU-ŠE-^{1}mil-⌜ki!⌝-x[ ]
9! [IGI ^{1}. .] -KUR-a-a

ADD 467 (AR 383) Obv 1' [. . . . .] ri . . .]
2' [. . . . .-r]e!-e ina KUR LÚ-⌜NIGIR!⌝-[É.GAL]
7' [. . .! ú]-piš-ma ^{1}EN-BÀD LÚ-GAL-⌜É⌝ [. .]!
8' [. . . . .]-MEŠ i-zi!-rip i-si-q[i] (U)
10' (end) la-[áš-šú]
11' (end) ina] ma-te-[ma]!
Rev 2' IGI ^{1}mu-L[AL]-aš-[šur . .]x[. . .]
3' IGI ^{1}še-⌜lu!⌝-bu [. . .]x x[. . .] (U)
4' IGI ^{1}[. .]!-aš+šur [. b]u . . .]
5' [IGI $^{1.d}$NIN!].GAL-MU-SUM-na [. . .]
6' [IGI ^{1}. .]-ba-⌜a⌝-nu LÚ- . . . .]!

ADD 468 (AR 439) Obv 1 NA$_4$-KIŠIB ^{1}⌜PAB⌝-ia-⌜qar⌝ LÚ*-2-ú ša ⌜URU-arrap!-ḫa!⌝[O]!
cylinder seal impression
2 [. . . .] 10 ⌜x⌝-a-ni! 1 GIŠ-SAR ⌜2⌝ [. . .]
3 [. . . .]⌜x x⌝ PAB 3 GIŠ-SAR-MEŠ
4 [e-nu ša A-ME]Š! ⌜É!⌝ LÚ*!-NU.GIŠ.SAR O!
5 [ina ŠÀ-bi] ú-piš-ma ^{1}PAB-ia-⌜ba⌝-ba
6 [ina ŠÀ 1] me! **URUDU**-MEŠ O! a!-na! ša-az-bu!-si
7 š[a! LÚ*]-⌜ḫu!⌝-ub-te! ša LÚ*-⌜SUKKAL!⌝ ina UGU
8 GIŠ-MÁ GUB-u-ni OK
12 [d]e!-nu DUG$_4$.DUG$_4$-bu
14 [lu-u] ⌜^{1}PAB⌝-ia-ba-ba ⌜:⌝ DUMU-MEŠ-[su]
Edge uninscribed
Rev 1! [lu-u DUMU-DUMU-MEŠ-šú] lu-u [PAB-MEŠ-šú]
2! [ša ina de]-ni!-šú! ⌜DUG$_4$!⌝.DU[G$_4$ . . .]!
3! [. . .(.)] ⌜lu!⌝ qu . . . .]!
4 [kas-pu a-na 10]-MEŠ ⌜a-na⌝ [E]N-MEŠ-šú G[UR.RA]
5 [IGI ^{1}. . .]-da!-a LÚ*!-m[u-. . .]
6 [IGI ^{1}. . .]-⌜ku⌝ LÚ*!-šá!-[. . . .]
7 [IGI 1. . . .]-⌜a!⌝ IGI ^{1}⌜e!-ni!-DINGIR!⌝

ADD 468 (AR 439) Rev 8 [IGI ^{1}. . .]-⸢APIN⸣-eš IGI $^{1.d}$UTU!-⸢x⸣
9 [IGI ^{1}. . .]-⸢i! LÚ*!-ḪAL!⸣
10 [IGI ^{1}. .]⸢x x⸣LÚ*!-A!.BA! ša! ⸢x x⸣
11 [IGI ^{1}. .]⸢x x⸣x LÚ*-A.[BA š]a URU-arrap-ḫa
12 [IGI ^{1}. .]⸢x x x x⸣
2 stamp seal impressions (no rulings)
15 LÚ*-GAR.KUR URU-ḫal!-zi!-[AD.BAR]

ADD 469 (AR 407) Obv 1 [. . . . .] ^{1}ur-bu-ru sic
2 [. . . . . LÚ]-⸢ÀLAD!⸣ šá URU-kar-^{d}U+GUR
3 [. . . . . K]UR-ga-su-pi

--!

unused space for fingernail(!) impressions

--!

4 [(.). . . . . . .] ú-šal-li šá ⸢KA⸣ [. .]-tar!
5 [. . . . . . .] ⸢a⸣-ki-su SUḪUR ^{1}ḫa-am!-[illegible] . .(.)-r]u! (U*)
6 [. . . . .][illegible] -MEŠ [illegible] di mu [illegible] . . . .]
7 [. . . . .]⸢É!⸣.GAL! 2!-u! [. . . . .]
9 [. . . .]x É! [. . . . .] (U)
10 [. . .]⸢x⸣ SUḪUR ^{1}ma-[. . . . .]
11 [. .]-[illegible] ina kit! [. . . . . . . (. .)]
12 ⸢SUḪUR! qa?-bu!⸣-ri ša ⸢a!⸣-[. . . . .(. .)]
13 šá ŠE.BAR ina! ⸢ŠÀ!-bi!⸣ la! ú-še-[. .(.)-n]i!⸢É! 2!⸣ A[NŠE! ..]
14 ina EDIN [illegible]-te! É d[a! [illegible] k]iš É ta-ba-[. . .]
15 A.ŠÀ e-ru-šú ⸢la!⸣ né-mu!-lu! ŠE-NUMUN! ⸢ub⸣-bu-lu la i-[..]
16 SUḪUR ÍD-ú-la-ia šá KÁ-ir-kal-li PAB URU!-[. . .]
17 A.ŠÀ la-qé-e-te ina URU-za-ku-u-te šá KÁ-ir-k[al!-li]
18 ú-piš-ma ^{1}ḫar-ḫa-an-da-a LÚ-$^{d!}$ÀLAD! šá É D[UMU!-LUGAL]
19 TA* IGI ^{1}ur-bu-ru DUMU ^{1}li-pu-ú-gu ina Š[À . . .]!
20 ku-pa-a-te ina 5 MA.NA UD.DA ^{MÍ}ar-na!-ši-[. . .] (sic!)
21 MÍ-AMA ^{d}ÀLAD-MEŠ il-qi kas-pu kám-[mur . .] (sic!)
22 la né-mu-lum A.ŠÀ i-si-qi t[u!-a-ru . . . . .]
Rev 3 4 ITU ⸢ša⸣ ITU-NE ITU-KIN ina i-ga-[ri . . . .(.)] (sic!)
4 4 pu-⸢la!-a!-ni!⸣ SUM-an 5 MA.NA UD.DA 7 MA.[NA . . .(.)]
5 SUM-an ⸢ina de-ni⸣-šú DUG$_{4}$.DUG$_{4}$-ma zi-[illegible][. . . .]!

----

6 IGI ^{1}sa-[. .]!-id-qi ^{d}ÀLAD ša T[A*! . . .]
7 IGI ^{1}sa-s[a]-⸢lu!-u LÚ*!-2!-u!⸣ ša [illegible] . .]
8 IGI ^{1}DÙG.GA-sa-⸢la⸣-me LÚ*-⸢x x x x⸣[. . .]
9 IGI ^{1}ú-a-ú-a :! ⸢ak!⸣-[k]u-u!⸢šá!⸣ URU!-[. . .]
10 IGI ^{1}qu-a-qu-a :! qa-ri-bu šá! b[i]r-ti [. . .]
11 IGI ^{1}ḫal-li-ar-ra-ka-a ⸢:!⸣ KUR!.GI-MUŠEN šá KUR!-[illegible][. .]

ADD 469 (AR 407) Rev 12 IGI ^{1}MURUB$_{4}$!-ḫar-da-a-te! :! a!-dam-mu-mu al-[. . .]
13 ša DAM-sà ina UGU -ḫa-ta-a-te! šá! KUR!-kaš-ia-[. . .]
14 IGI ^{1}di-ib-ba-a- ga . . .]
15 [. . . . .(.)] ^{1}qa-[.] ⸢LÚ*!⸣-[. . . . .]
16 [. . . . .] ⸢ša⸣ qa ⸢la⸣ [. .]
17 [. . . . .(.)] GÌR!.NUN.NA ⸢šá!⸣ ka-le-⸢e!⸣[. .]
18 [. . . . . .(.)] qa ⸢su⸣ uḫ si ^{d}15 [0]
19 [. . . . . . .] LÚ*-GAR.KUR 0! EDIN

!

20 [. . . . .] DINGIR!-MEŠ
21 [ ] ⸢i/kám⸣
22 [ ] -bu!-⸢a/za⸣-a!

!

Edge 23 [-a-ti

ADD 471 (AR 167) Obv Beginning lost; unused space for stamp seal impressions

!

5' (end) URU-DÙG.GA-GIŠ.⸢MI!⸣-[. . . . .]
6' (end) LÚ-EN.NAM ⸢URU!⸣-[ar-pad-da]
8' (end) LÚ-ENG[AR 0!]
14' šá! LÚ-EN.NAM
19' TA* IGI ^{1}i-ka-ri TI-qí! kas-pu gam-mur (U)

ADD 472 (AR 101) Obv 1 [NA$_{4}$-KIŠIB ^{1}.]-⸢ki!-ki! LÚ*⸣-[. .(.)]
2 [. . . .(.)! E]N! URU-ŠE ta-da-ni

!

cylinder seal impression(!); on edge, impression of stamp seal

!

4 [a-di A].ŠÀ-MEŠ-šú a!-[di]! GIŠ-SAR-MEŠ-šú (U)
5 [a-di UN]-MEŠ-šú ina! ⸢qab!-si! šá! URU⸣-ak-[. . .]
7 [SUḪUR U]RU-ŠE-^{1}ta-ba-
8 [SUḪUR U]RU-ŠE-^{1}[[. .]]-u-te
9 [SUḪUR URU-Š]E-^{1}⸢lu!-u!⸣-PAB-MEŠ
10 [. . . .] -ka-na-a
11 [. URU]-ŠE!-^{1}NUMUN-ti-i (U)
12 [ú-piš-m]a! ^{1}mil-ki-ZÁLAG LÚ*-SAG ša ⸢MÍ!-KUR!⸣(U*)
13 [ina ŠÀ .] MA.NA KUG.GI il-q[í]
14 [kas-pu gam]-mur ta-ad!-din URU-ŠE [0]! (U)
15 [šú-a-tú! za-rip] laq-qi tu-a-r[u]
16 [de-e-nu! DUG$_{4}$.DUG$_{4}$] la-áš-šú (U)
18 [lu-u ^{1}.-k]i!-⸢ki!⸣ lu-u DUMU-[MEŠ-šú]

Edge uninscribed

Rev 1 [ša TA* ^{1}mil-ki-ZÁLAG! de]-e-nu DUG$_{4}$.DUG$_{4}$
2 [ub-ta-u-n]i! [b]i-lat MA.NA! KUG.UD 0! (U*)

ADD 472 (AR 101) Rev 3 [ina bur-ki]! ša ^{d}iš-tar ša NINA-[KI] (U*)
4 [GAR-a]n! kas-pu ana 10-MEŠ-te a-na EN-[MEŠ-šú]
5 [GUR].RA ina de-ni-šú DUG$_4$.DUG$_4$-ma! NU TI!-q[í]! (U*)
———— !
6 [IGI ^{1}]KA-DINGIR-KI-[a-a LÚ*]-3.U[$_5$]
7 [IGI ^{1}]am!-bu!-[. .]x
8 [IGI ^{1}t]ab!-URU-⌜a!-a!⌝ [IGI ^{1}]EN-URU!-KASKAL-PAB-PAB
9 [IGI $^{1.d}$]IM!--a!-⌜ni!⌝ [LÚ*]-qur-ZAG
10-12 names entirely obliterated
13! [IGI ^{1}]NUMUN-tú URU!-ḫa!-za!-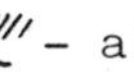- a!-[a]
14! [IGI ^{1}. .]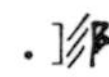-a! LÚ*-DAM.QAR
15! [IGI $^{1.d}$P]A!-SAG-iš!-ši (U)
16! [IGI ^{1}b]a-zu-zu LÚ*-ḫa-za-nu
17! [UR]U!-ŠE MÍ-É.GAL URU-la-ḫi-ra-a-a (U*)
18! (end) LÚ*-gu-gal sic ()
19' [. 
21' [ITU-KI]N UD-19!()-KAM

ADD 473 (AR 90) Obv 1 (end) ^{1}ḫa ru ra [nu!]
2 (end) iš-k[u]n! (sic; cf. U)
———— !
11 fingernail impressions
———— !
6 PAB 4 LÚ*!-ZI-MEŠ sa ^{1}ḫ[a-ru-ra-nu] O!
7 
8 entirely destroyed
9 [. . . . . . A].⌜ŠÀ⌝.G[A-MEŠ]
10 [. . . . .(.)]⌜bi⌝ a-du
11 [. . . . . . T]I!-qi-ú O!
12 [tu-a-ru de-e-nu] DUG$_4$.DUG$_4$ O!
13 [la-áš-šú! man-nu] ša ina ar-kát UD-me O! (U)
14 [i-za-qu-pa-a]n!-ni : lu-u ^{1}ḫa-ru-[ra-nu]
15 [lu-u ^{1}sa-l]i-la-a-nu
17 [lu-u PAB]-MEŠ!-šú-nu lu-u DUMU-MEŠ! ŠE[Š!-MEŠ-šú-nu] (U)
18 [lu-u LÚ*!-ḫ]a-za-na-šú-nu lu-u [. . . . .]
19 [lu-u I]M!.RI.A KI+MIN KI+MIN [. . .]!
Edge!22 [de-nu] DUG$_4$.DUG$_4$ ⌜i⌝-[gar-ru-ni]
Rev 1-2 destroyed
3! [. . . . .] ki u [. . . .]
4! [. . . .]-MEŠ! la laq-qi-[u! . . .]
5! [. . . .]-mur! ú-ma-a . . .]
6! [. . . . . a-na EN-šú [GUR.RA]
7! [ina de-ni-šú] DUG$_4$.DUG$_4$-ma la [i-laq-qi]!

ADD 473 (AR 96) Rev 8! [IGI ^{1}U+GUR-š]al!-lim-an-ni LÚ*-GAL-[. . .]
9! [IGI ^{1}. . .] ⌜LÚ*!⌝-GAL-⌜sa!⌝-. . .]
10! [IGI ^{1}AN.GAL-me]-si! LÚ*!-⌜rak!-su!⌝ [. . .]
11! [IGI $^{1.d}$IM-k]a-šir [. . . .]
12! [IGI . . . . .] [. . .]
13! [IGI . . . . . .][. . . .]
14! IGI ^{1}. . . . .]
15! DUMU URU-N[INA!-KI]
16! IGI ^{1}ba-qu-[. . . . .]
17! IGI $^{1.d}$IM-tak-lak L[Ú*!-. . .]
18! (end) ^{1}bal-t[i!-. .]
L.E. 1 [. . . . .] i-ta-ṣu

ADD 474 (AR 96a) Obv 1'! [. . . (.)] lu! [. . . . . .]
2'! [man-nu] šá ina KUR! NIM!.MA![. . . .]
3'! ⌜ša!⌝ e-la-an-ni lu-u ^{1}ḫa-ru-ra-a-⌜nu!⌝
10'! TA*! ⌜^{1}DUMU.UŠ-a-a⌝ ù DUMU-MEŠ-šú (U)
13'! i-si-tu a-di ⌜a/za!⌝-[. . . . .]
Rev 4 DUG-a-gan-ni sad-ru ⌜NAG! DUMU!⌝-[šú GAL . . .]
5 GÍBIL DUMU.⌜MÍ-su⌝ GAL-tú TA*! 3BÁN! ÚŠ!-⌜ERIN⌝
10 IGI $^{1.d}$U+GUR-šal-lim-a-ni LÚ-
11 IGI ^{1}AN.GAL-me-si LÚ-rak!-s[u]!

ADD 475 (AR 525) Obv 2 [iš-ku]n! ṣu-pur ^{1}DINGIR-SU!
————————————————!
5 fingernail impressions
————————————————!
4 [. . . . .(.)] ^{1}man-nu-GIM(wr.BAN!)-PAB-MEŠ
5 [. . . . . .(.)] di
6 [. . . . . . .(.)] ⌜1⌝ MA.NA KUG.UD
Rev 1' [. . . . .] $^{1.d}$30!-. . .]
2' [. . . . . .] LÚ*-TUR ša $^{1.d}$AMAR.UTU-MAN!-P[AB] (U)
3' [IGI ^{1}.-m]u!-u-a DUMU URU-NINA-a O!
4' [IGI ^{1}. .]- (blank) i
5' [IGI ^{1}]ITU-KIN-a-a EN- -MEŠ
6' [IGI] $^{1!}$UD-ši- (blank) e
7' [IG]I $^{1.d}$PA-MU-iš-kun
8' [L]Ú*-A.BA ṣa-bit ṭup-pi
10' [IGI ^{1}-si-i O! ša-GÌR+2
11' [IGI . . r]a!-ni-i LÚ*-Ì[R . . .] (U)
Edge 12' [. . . . . LU]GAL!
13' [. . . . . . .] EN-iá LÚ*!-[. . .]

ADD 481 (AR 162) Obv 3' SUḪUŠ wr. [sign]
4' (end) LÚ*-⌜šá!⌝-[. . .]
7' (end) [NAG]!
8' [3BÁN ZÀ].ḪI.LI-SAR a-di KÁ!.GA[L! . . . .]
9' [ina K]A! EME-šú i-laq-qut a!-[. .]
10' [. GI]Š-BÁN-šú ú-mal-lu-u-n[i]!
Rev 3 IGI ^{1}EN-KALAG-an LÚ-A-É.GAL sic (cf. U)
4 ša É-UŠ-MEŠ-te IGI ^{1}[.]-⌜SUM!-A!⌝
5 LÚ-ME.ME ša ina IGI ^{1}aš+šur-MU-⌜DÙ!⌝[pa-qid-d]u!-ni!
6 IGI ^{1}EN-PAB-ir LÚ-ḪAL! š[a! A]-MAN
7 IGI ^{1}GIŠ-PA-šu-al-di-i LÚ*-qur!-[bu-ti]!
8 IGI ^{1}bar-ruq LÚ-TIN ša ⌜É A!⌝-[MAN]!
9 [IGI ^{1}DINGIR]-a-a-MAN-DÙ O! LÚ*-ŠÀ!.TAM! [sign]]
L.E. 1 [. . . . -^{d}]AG! LÚ*-AG[RIG . .]
3 [LÚ-GAR].KUR É-z[a!-ma-ni]

ADD 486 (AR 198) Obv 1' [. . . . . .]! laq-qi-⌜ú⌝
4' [i-z]a-qu-pa-a-ni lu-u ^{1}ERIM!-MEŠ-SIG
8' [GUR.R]A! a-na

ADD 489 (AR 382) Obv 1' [. . . . .] šú [. .]!
2' [ina ŠÀ-bi . MA.N]A! KUG.UD il-[qí]
4' [GIŠ-SA]R! šu-a-te za-ár-pi! la-qi (U)
Rev 4 [. . . . .][sign] -⌜an!⌝-ni
6 [. . . . . . . M]A!.NA!

ADD 491 (AR 58) Obv 2a cylinder seal impression
3 MÍ!-⌜ú!⌝-ḫi!-ma-a (U*)
4 [MÍ-šú ša $^{1.d}$E]N?-⌜DÙ!-uš!⌝
5 [. . . .(.)][sign] lu! [. .]
6 [. . . .] sa [sign][. . .]
Rest of Obverse destroyed
Edge broken away
Rev 1' [. . . .] GÌR+2! [sign][. .]
2' [. . . .[sign] áš! [sign] . .]
3' [mim-ma TA*] mim-ma
4' [la i]-⌜da!⌝-bu-ub
5' [TA* pa-a]n! a-ḫa-iš
6' [uṭ]-ṭu!-ru DUG$_4$.DUG$_4$ la-áš-šú
7' IGI ^{1}su-ra-[ra]-a!-te

ADD 492 (AR 432) Obv 1' [. . . . . .] nu [.] [. . . . .]

2' [. .]-⸢li!⸣ ša URU-arba-ìl [. . .]!

4' [ina ŠÀ] 80! MA.NA URUDU-MEŠ 2! ANŠE ŠE!-PAD!-MEŠ a-ki pa-ša!-[ri] (U*)

5' [i-z]i!-rip i-si-qi

7' DI.KUD sic

8' UD-me a-ṣa-ti sic

11' [šá de-nu] DUG$_4$.DUG$_4$

12' [ub-ta-']u!-u-ni

13' [a-na ^{d}15 ša] URU!-arba-ìl

15' [ina] DI.KUD!-šú

ADD 494 (AR 618) Obv destroyed(!)

Rev! 1 [šá d]e-e-nu DU[G$_4$.DUG$_4$]

2 [T]A* ^{1}mil-ki-ZÁLAG DUMU-M[EŠ-šú]

9 [IGI ^{1}.] -'e-e-i LÚ-3.U$_5$-šú ša [. . . .]!

10 [IGI ^{1}qur]-di!-U+GUR LÚ*-GAL-kal-la[p . . .]!

ADD 498 (AR 164) Obv 2' [lu-u DUMU-DUMU-M]EŠ!-šú-nu lu-u DUMU!-P[AB!-MEŠ-šú-nu]

6' MAŠ.SU sad-ru sic

9' (end) LÚ-EN.N[AM! URU-šú SUM-an]

10' bi-lat ZA.GÌN ḫi-ip

Rev 4' IGI ^{1}⸢li⸣-[qi]-pu [. . . .] (U)

ADD 500 (AR 615) Obv 1' [. . . . . .(.)! z]a-rip TI-qí tu-a-ru O!

2' [de-e-nu! DU]G$_4$.DUG$_4$ la-áš-šú man-nu šá O! (U)

3' [ina ur-kiš! ina ma]-te-e-ma lu-u LÚ!-ERIM-MEŠ šú-nu-te (U)

4' [lu-u DUMU-ME]Š!-šú-nu lu-u DUMU-DUMU-O!-šu-nu (U*)

6' [ša de]-⸢e⸣-nu DUG$_4$.DUG$_4$ É! ^{1}ka-da-la-ni (U)

12' (end) 10-MEŠ O! (U)

Rev 2 IGI $^{1.d}$PA-u-a IGI ^{1}man-nu-ki-i-^{d}PA!

3 end possibly IGI ^{1}⸢i-lu-KI-ia!⸣, but broken

4 [IG]I ^{1}GIN-MAN-te-DINGIR IGI ^{1} -qi!-i

7 [IGI ^{1}. .]-su-ur-⸢ri!⸣

8 [. . . . .]-ni! 2! URU-šu-ra-a-a

9 [IGI ^{1}. .]-ṭu-ru IGI ^{1}⸢DÙ⸣-IGI.LAL ⸢ÌR!⸣-MEŠ

11 (end) IGI ^{1}Ì!.GÁL-DINGIR-MEŠ

13 [IGI ^{1}. .]-i! 2! URU!-i!-ni!-KUR? IGI [^{1}]a-zi-DINGIR

14 [IGI ^{1}. . .]-a 2! URU-ḫi-di-ni-ba

15 (end) 2 URU-ŠE-^{1} -du

16 [. . . . . . .]

ADD 503 (AR 614) Obv 1' [.] [ ]
6' lu-u ^{1}de-ti-EN-DU!-k[a]!
7' lu-u DUMU O! lu-u DUMU-DUMU-š[ú] sic
9' TA*! not TA
Rev 2 i-šá-ka-an kas-pi! ina 10-MEŠ (U)
4 i-da-bu-bu sic
5 i-la-qi ⌜ EN de-e-nu O!

6 IGI ^{1}ki-ṣir-aš+šur LÚ*-mu!-ki[l!-KUŠ-PA-MEŠ]
8 IGI $^{1.d}$PA-⌜NUMUN!⌝-AŠ [. . .]

ADD 504 (AR 569) Obv 1 NA$_4$-KIŠIB ^{1}IGI-^{d}PA!-bi-[. . .]! sic
3 NA$_4$-KIŠIB $^{1.d}$PA!-še-zib-⌜a!⌝-[ni]!
4 NA$_4$-KIŠIB ^{1}DI-mu- [. . .]!
5 NA$_4$-KIŠIB $^{1.d}$UTU-ku!-
6a ———————————————!
1[+n] stamp seal impression[s]
———————————————!
Rev 5' IGI ^{1}
9' [lim]-mu ^{1}L[UGAL!-. . . .]
10' ⌞ki⌟-iṣ!-ri

ADD 505 (AR 613) Obv! 1' [. . .] [. . . . .]
2' [TA*]! IGI $^{1.d}$PA-[. . .] (U)
3' [i]l!-qi! kas-[pu gam-mur ta-din] (U)
4' [É] ⌜UN!⌝-MEŠ [šu-a-te zar-pu]
Rev! 1' [. . .^{1}]$^{.⌜d!⌝}$P[A!-. . . .]
2' [DUM]U!-MEŠ-šú [šá de-nu DUG$_4$.DUG$_4$] (U)
3' [TA* ^{1}]ni-nu-a-[a u DUMU-MEŠ-šú] (U)
4' [ub]-ta-u-ni [. . . . .]
5' [. .]-⌜a!⌝-a! ta-da-[. . . .]
6' [.] MA.NA KUG.GI ⌜a!⌝-[na . . . .]
7' [kas-p]u! a-na [. . . . .]

ADD 506 (AR 612) Obv 1' [. . . . .]x x[. . .] tú!
2' [. . . . .]x x[. . ta]-din!
3' [. . šu-a-tu zar-pu la]-⌜qí!⌝-'u!-u!
4' [tu-a-ru de-e-nu DUG$_4$].DUG$_4$!
5' [la-áš-šú man-nu ša .] -u-ni O!
7' [. . . . . .] LÚ*-2-⌜e⌝ O!
Edge 8' [. . . . .] DUMU-DUMU-šú
9' [lu-u L]Ú*!-EN.NAM ša URU-arrap-ḫa

ADD 506 (AR 612) Rev 3 [kas-pu] la O! ga-mur la-a ta!-din! (U*)
4 [. . .] šu!-a-ti! la ta-din
5 [.]! MA.NA KUG.UD ina bur-ki ^{d}15 (U)
6 [ša]! URU-ni-nu-a i-šá-kan
7 [. M]A.NA
9 [IGI] ^{1}LUGAL-IGI.LAL-a-ni LÚ*!(not LÚ)-qur-ZAG
10 [IGI ^{1}]DI-mu-EN-la-áš-O! LÚ*!-3.[U_5] (U)
11 [IGI ^{1}. . . .]-⸢ni!⸣ [. . . .]

ADD 509 (AR 609) Rev 2 TA* IGI!(text U) ^{1}IM-U+GUR-DU!-
6 IGI ^{1}ab-bu-. . . .]
7 IGI ^{1}DINGIR-a-⸢a!⸣-[. . .]

ADD 510 (AR 608) Obv 1' [. . . . .]
2' [ú-piš-ma ^{1}. .]-SU-ba O!
3' [ina ŠÀ . MA.N]A KUG!.UD! il-qi (U)
Rev 1' [IGI ^{1}. . . .]
3' [IGI ^{1}. . . L]Ú*!-GIGIR ša GÌR+2-ME!
4' [IGI ^{1}. . .]-e LÚ*-GIGIR (sic)
5' [IGI ^{1}.(.)]-⸢ni!⸣-i (spaced)
6' [IGI . . . .] a -di-15

ADD 513 (AR 392) Obv 2a cylinder seal impression; on edge, stamp seal impression
Rev 1' [IGI ^{1}.]x-ṭu! URU!-[. .-a-a]
2' IGI [^{1}.]-a'! URU-[. . .-a-a]
3' (blank) DUMU ^{1}li-[. . .]
4' sic
5' [IG]I ^{1}a-du-nu KUR-ḫal!-p[a!-a-a]
6' PAB 5 ⸢TA*! URU⸣-ar-gu-⸢ú!⸣-nu
7' [IGI ^{1}. . .š]ad-du- u+a!
8' [LÚ*-A.BA ṣa-b]it ṭup-pi
9' [. . . KU]R!-ṣi-du-nu-a-a
10' [. . .] PAB! 3! TA*! ša ina UGU na-ḫal
11' [IGI ^{1}aš+š]ur!-MAN-PAB LÚ*-sa-si-nu
12' [T]A*! URU-UŠ-ANŠE

ADD 514 (AR 386) Obv! 6' [TA*] IGI ^{1}ki-ṣir!-15 ina Š[À!-bi] (U)
7' [. MA.N]A! ⸢KUG!.UD!⸣ il-qi x[. .]

ADD 515 (AR 408) Obv Beginning destroyed; (unused?) seal space

―――――――――――――――――――― !

1' [É . AN]ŠE A.ŠÀ.GA

2' [. . .] URU-ŠE-^{1}an-da-ra-ni

3' [. . .]-MEŠ É a-na URU-da-ri-g[i]!

4' [. . .] É 3 ANŠE É ši-q[i! . .]

6' [LÚ*-DIB-KUŠ-PA]-MEŠ [

ADD 516 (AR 410) Obv Beginning destroyed; then seal space with faint stamp seal impression; no ruling

2' [. . . URU-DÙG.G]A!-e-te

3' [. . ^{1}aš+šu]r!-ga-⸢ru⸣-u-a-ni-ri

4' [.(.)] URU!-kap!-r[i]!-^{1}⸢bir⸣-ta-a-a

5' [. URU-kul-i]m!-me-er-ra

6' sic

7' [SUḪUR A].ŠÀ ša ^{1}aš+šur-g[a-ru-u-a-ni-ri]

Rev 1 [SUḪUR A].ŠÀ ša $^{1.d}$IM-[

2 [SUḪUR É] ^{1}gi-[

ADD 517 (AR 391) Obv 1' [. . . . .(.)] di

4' [il-qi! k]as-pu gam-mur ta-din

6' sic

10' [lu-u DUMU-ME]Š!-šú-nu lu-u [. .]

ADD 518 (AR 409) Obv 1' [SUḪUR]! A.ŠÀ ša ^{1}. . . . . . .]

2' [i-n]a! UGU [. . . . .]

3' SUḪUR A.ŠÀ [. . . . .]

Rev 1' [a-š]ib! URU-[. . . . .] (U)

2' [a]!-na EN-MEŠ-[šú . . . . .] (U)

3' 0! DUG$_4$.DUG$_4$-ma [. . . .] (U)

――――――――――――――――――――

4' [IGI ^{1}]mu-né-pi-i[š!-DINGIR . . .]

6' [IGI ^{1}][ ]

ADD 519 (AR 369) Obv 1' [. . . . .][. . .]!

2' [. . . . .] 5! GIŠ-I[G!-MEŠ]

5' [. . . . .(.) .]-di SUḪUR ⸢su!⸣-qa-qi

6' [. . . . .(.) t]u-piš-ma

7' [. . . . .] GAL ša U.U!

8' [TA* IGI $^{1.d}$P]A!-šal-lim ina ŠÀ-bi (U)

9' [. MA.NA! KUG.U]D! ša URU-gar-ga-miš

11' [. . . . šu]-⸢a!⸣-te

ADD 519 (AR 369) Obv 13' [man-nu ša (ina) ur-ki-i]š! ina ma-te-ma
Rev 1 [TA* MÍ. . . ub-ta]!-'u-u-ni (U)
2 [. MA.NA KUG.G]I! ina bur-ki ᵈiš-tar (U*)
3 [a-ši-bat URU]-ni!-na!-a! i-šak-[kan] (U)
10 [IGI ¹ . .]-⌜i!⌝
12 [. . . . .] O!
13 [. . . . .]-⌜LAL!⌝

ADD 520 (AR 411) Obv 1' [. . . . .] qa! 1 ⌜BÁN!⌝ URUDU O!
2' [. . . . . . . i]a-u-tú sic
one line blank
3' [. . . . . . A].ŠÀ ša ¹aš+šur-NUMUN-DÙ
4' [. . . . . .] ¹PAB-la-maš-ši LÚ*-GIŠ.GIGIR
5' [. . . . . . in]a ŠÀ-bi
6' [il-qi! kas-pu gam]-mur ta-din-ni
7' [.-MEŠ šu-a-tu zar-p]u! la-qi-ú
10' [lu-u ¹. .] -PAB-MEŠ
11' [lu-u DUMU-MEŠ]-⌜ŠEŠ!⌝-MEŠ-šú
Rev 1 [ša TA* ¹PAB-la-maš]-ši! DUMU-MEŠ-šú
2 [de-e-nu DUG_4.D]UG_4! ub-ta-AN-u-[ni] (sic)
5 [GUR.RA ina] de-e!-ni-šú DUG_4.DUG_4-ma sic (cf. U)
6a ———————————————————!
7 IGI ⌜¹. . . . . IGI]! ¹aš+šur-NUMUN-DÙ (U)
8 IGI ¹[. . . . . IGI! ¹]·⌜ᵈ⌝ŠÚ-ḪAL-a-ni (U)
9 [IGI ¹. . .(.). IGI ¹.] -na-a-a
two lines blank
10 [. . . . .]-a-a

ADD 521 (AR 385) Obv 1' [. . . . . .] -qa-ba-a-te
2' [. . . . . .] -an-ni
3' [. . . . . .]-ba! (U)
4' [. . . . . .] URU-ṣi-ib!-te
7' [TA* IGI ¹. . .] -ra! il-qí
Edge 8' [kas-pu ga-mur t]a!-din-ni
Rev 6 [lu mim-ma-nu]-⌜šú!⌝ qur!-[bu . . .]

ADD 522 (AR 380) Obv 1' ⌜6 ANŠE! A!⌝.[ŠÀ
2' ina URU-ḫa-[. . . .]
4' SUḪUR MÍbi-s[i!- (U)
6' ú-piš-ma ¹M[U!-. . .]
8' [TA* IGI ¹]⌜ᵈ!⌝IM!-. . .]

ADD 522 (AR 380) L.E.1 . . .]x SAG 2 ANŠE ŠE-PAD šá! [. . . .

ADD 524 (AR 405) Obv 1'] A!.⸢ŠÀ!⸣ [
2'] ina! ŠÀ! ub- -a-ti!
3' AN]ŠE! A.ŠÀ! ina ŠÀ! GABA! SUḪU[R (U)
4' SUḪUR KASKAL š]a! ana! URU!-ŠÀ-URU [(U)
6' ANŠE A].ŠÀ SUḪUR um!-[me (U)
7' A].ŠÀ! SU[ḪUR! (U)

ADD 536 (AR 666) Obv destroyed!
Rev! 1' [. .] ^{1}ḫar-ma-ki
2' [. .]sa-ma!-a-ti (U)
3'![. . .] IGI! $^{1!}$PAB-AŠ (U)
4'![. . . .] IGI! $^{1!}$ZI-PAB (U)
5'![. . . . IG]I! $^{1.d}$PA̭SUM-PAB-MEŠ
6'![. . . . .]

ADD 540 (AR 667) Obv 1' [. . . . .] [. . .]; two lines blank
3' [. . . . .] gab ba [. . . .]
Rev 3' [IGI ^{1}sa-s]i!-i LÚ-ḫa-[za-nu . . .]

ADD 545 Obv 1' [. . . . . .] ^{1}ri!-[. . . .]
2' [. . . . .] URUDU! il-q[i]!
3' [man-nu ša . .] i-da-nu-[ni]
4' [LÚ ú]-⸢še!⸣-ṣa! IGI ^{1}. . .]
5' [IGI ^{1}]PAB-la-mur LÚ*-[. .]
6' [IGI] $^{1!}$mar-di!-[i]
Rev 1 [IGI ^{1}]e-še!-ra-[a-a]
2 [IGI ^{1}]sa-me-⸢ku!⸣[0]
3 [IGI ^{1}]ZU-^{d}[. .]
4 [ITU-. UD]-18!-K[ÁM]

ADD 546 (letter!) Obv 1' [. . . . .-M]EŠ! a-⸢du!⸣ [. .(.)]!
2' [. . . . . an]-ni-u ša! L[UGAL]!
3' [be-lí iš-pur-an]-ni! ^{1}EN-lu-T[I.LA]
4' [. . . . .] ša ^{1}aš+šur-ina!-ŠU-[. .]
5' [. . . . . a]n!-nu-te É-ŠU+[2 0]
6' [. . . . . .] a-nu-tú
7' [. . . . . . e]p!-šú!-u-ni [. .]
8' [. . . . .] ša [. . .]

ADD 546 Obv 9' [. . . . . . .] ÌR! ^{1}ki-ṣ[ir!-DN]
10' [. . . . . . .] DUMU ^{1}aš+šur-ina-Š[U!-. .]
one line erased
Edge & Rev. totally destroyed

ADD 547 (AR 603) Obv 1 [NA$_4$-KISIB $^{1.d}$]U+GUR!-⌜ZU!⌝ (U)
2 [EN . . . . . ta-da-n]i? (U*)
Rev 1' [. . . . . . .] $^{d!}$gu!-la (U)
2' [. . . . . . . LÚ*-A-B]A! É-DINGIR
5' [IGI] ^{1}LUG[AL!-. .] ⌜LÚ*!⌝-mu-kil!-⌜PA!⌝-MEŠ
7' [IGI ^{1}]ul!-lu IGI 1-O! (U)

ADD 548 (AR 601) Obv 2a ————————————!
2[+n] stamp seal impressions
Rev 1' [IGI ^{1}. . . .] LÚ*!-x[. . .]
2' [IGI ^{1}man-nu-ki-URU]-⌜ni!-nu!-a!⌝ [. . .]
3' [IGI ^{1}. . .]⌜x x x x⌝ ša A-MAN
8' [IGI ^{1}. . . ///-AŠ!-PAB^{MEŠ}

ADD 550 (AR 602) Obv 8' [la i-la]q!-q[í]! (spaced)
————————————!
Rev 1' [IGI ^{1}man-nu-ki]-⌜i!⌝-LUGAL

ADD 555 (oracle query, no legal text!)
3'] lu-u ⌜za!⌝-[
4' lu]-ú! GIŠ!-GIGIR! [
5'] lu-ú /// [
6']-⌜tin!⌝-ni [
7']/// -a-⌜a!⌝[
9' l]u!-ú [

ADD 679 (AR 292) Obv 2 4 TÚG-nik-si du[l!-. .]
4 ina pa-an ^{1}ur-da-⌜a!⌝[0]
7 ár!-ḫiš ep-pa-pa-a[l]! ()
Rev 4 ^{1}  -li-[. .]

ADD 801 (AR 65a) Obv 1 NA$_4$-KIŠIB $^{1.}$[$^{d!}$EN]-A-AŠ
2 LÚ-GAL-a- /// . .]-ri šá URU-tar-bu-si-ba
3 EN LÚ*-U[N-ME]Š ta-da-a-ni
————————————
two stamp seal impressions(!)
————————————

ADD 801 (AR 65a) Obv 4! $^{1!}$[. . . . .]

16 DUG$_4$.DUG$_4$ [la-áš-šú man-nu šá ina ur-ki]š!

19 lu-u DUMU-MEŠ-šú :! DUMU-DUMU-MEŠ-šú (U)

Rev 2! [. . . . . EN]-MEŠ-šú

break of 3 lines

---!

6! [IGI ^{1}. . . . .]-nu

8! [IGI ^{1}. . . LÚ*-GAL-ki-ṣ]ir! šá MAN

10' [IGI ^{1}sa-ka]n!-nu LÚ*-mu-ki[l-PA-MEŠ]

11' (end) LÚ*-2-[u] (U)

12' [š]a LÚ*!-GAL-ú-rat! [0] (U)

13' IGI! ^{1}aš+šur!-DINGIR!-a-a DUMU! ^{1}MAN-DÙ! (U)

14' IGI $^{1.d!}$U.GUR(wr. 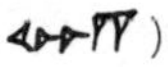)-MAN-PAB

15' ⌜ša!⌝ LÚ*!-MAḪ!-URU [šá UR]U-tar-bu-si-ba (U*)

rest as in AR

MONOGRAPHS ON THE ANCIENT NEAR EAST

Volume 1

Fascicle 1: A. Falkenstein, *The Sumerian Temple City* (1954)
Introduction and Translation by M. deJ. Ellis. 21 pp., $2.30

Fascicle 2: B. Landsberger, *Three Essays on the Sumerians* (1943-1945)
Introduction and Translation by M. deJ. Ellis. 18 pp., $2.00

Fascicle 3: I. M. Diakonoff, *Structure of Society and State in Early Dynastic Sumer* (1959)
Summary and translation of selected passages by the author
Introduction by M. Desrochers. 16 pp., $1.80

Fascicle 4: B. Landsberger, *The Conceptual Autonomy of the Babylonian World* (1926)
Translation by Th. Jacobsen, B. Foster and H. von Siebenthal
Introduction by Th. Jacobsen. 16 pp., $1.80

The famous programmatic article by Benno Landsberger, "Die Eigenbegrifflichkeit der Babylonischen Welt," was a manifesto which "insisted on the necessity of studying Mesopotamian culture for its own sake, in its own terms, and within its own system of values": as Jacobsen notes, it was "under the banner of Eigenbegrifflichkeit [that] Landsberger . . . may be said to have made Assyriology for the first time an autonomous discipline." The article is here made available in a masterly translation by Jacobsen, based on two initial drafts by Foster and von Siebenthal: it provides an accurate and sensitive reading by another intellectual giant in the field, who was himself a long time personal friend of the author. The introduction, published originally as an obituary, gives a brief and penetrating assessment of Landsberger's life work.

Fascicle 5: M. Liverani, *Three Amarna Essays* (1965-1972)
Translation and Introduction by Matthew L. Jaffe. 34 pp., $3.60

A translation of three articles originally published in Italian: "Pharaoh's Letters to Rib-Adda" (1971). "Social Implications in the Politics of Abdi-Aširta of Amurru" (1965), and "'Irrational' Elements in the Amarna Trade" (1972). The three articles translated here underscore Mario Liverani's commitment to a balanced, "global" approach to Ancient Near Eastern history. Narrow philological or other "antiquarian" attitudes are eschewed in favor of including anthropological, socio-economic, and other typological models in the study of Near Eastern civilizations in this period. Liverani presents certain political and diplomatic facets of Ancient Near Eastern history, particularly the second half of the Second Millennium B.C. in Syria, in their proper societal settings with a regard for such diverse perspectives as customs and ideology, market theory, religion, nomadism versus sedentarism, geography and literary criticism.

Fascicle 6: P. Matthiae, *Ebla in the Period of the Amorite Dynasties* (1974)
Translation and Introduction by Matthew L. Jaffe. 36 pp., 20 pl., $7.50

This 1974 article on the archaeological documentation from Tell Mardikh came on the heels of the major discovery of the great archive of Ebla. As such, it provided the setting against which the discovery can best be appreciated, and it retains a classic value which makes its present English publication especially useful. Many new photographic illustrations add to the documentary value of the initial publication.

Fascicle 7: G. Pettinato, *Old Canaanite Texts from Ebla* (1975)
Translation and Introduction by Matthew L. Jaffe. 17 pp. $2.00

This article contains the first grammatical description of Eblaite, a new Semitic language attested in the texts from Tell Mardikh-Ebla. The article was first published in Italian in 1975 and is here published for the first time in English translation. It provides ample grammatical documentation from the first archive discovered in 1974 at Ebla, numbering 42 tablets. It also provides the first assessment of the linguistic and historical evidence of the texts.

Volume 2

Fascicle 1: C. Saporetti, *The Status of Women in the Middle Assyrian Period*
Translation and Introduction by Beatrice Boltze-Jordan. 20 pp., $2.50

A synthesis of data pertinent to the situation of the woman in the Middle-Assyrian period, drawn from the laws and economic texts. Her situation within family and society is discussed through the various phases of her life—as unmarried and as a married woman, as divorcée and widow. The resulting picture shows an unusual degree of harshness in the limitations placed on her personal freedom.